35 Questions Christians Ask Scientists
Paul Wallace

Publication sponsored by:
William and Charlotte Ellis, Lexington, Ky.
Cynthia D. Green, Avondale Estates, Ga.
R. Mark Green, Avondale Estates, Ga.
David Jordan and Beth Jackson-Jordan, Decatur, Ga.
William and Judy Neal, Fayetteville, Ga.
Roy Runyan Jr., Jonesboro, Ark.
Kenneth and Lisa Rust, Lumberton, N.C.
Martha Strader, Granada Hills, Cal.
Brent Walker, Falls Church, Va.
Tim and Lynda Willis, Clemson, S.C.

© 2022
Published in the United States by Nurturing Faith Inc., Macon Ga.,
Nurturing Faith is a book imprint of Good Faith Media (www.goodfaithmedia.org).

Library of Congress Cataloging-in-Publication Data is available.

ISBN: #978-1-63528-202-3
All rights reserved. Printed in the United States of America.

All scripture citations are taken from the New Revised Standard Version (NRSV)
unless otherwise indicated.

Contents

Introduction
All the way down and all the way out
v

Question 1
Since you are a Baptist minister, are you a creationist?
1

Question 2
How do you explain the Old Testament story of creation with your scientific methods?
4

Question 3
How were you able to study science in school and allow room for your faith to grow?
7

Question 4
Why do scientists think their calculations for the age of the universe (almost 13.8 billion years) and the size of the universe (billions and billions of light-years) are better than beliefs based on the Bible?
10

Question 5
Taking into account scientific calculations for the size and expansion and age of the cosmos, what is your view of the spiritual significance of humans in the universe?
13

Question 6
How have you furthered your faith through your work as a scientist?
16

Question 7
What does the Bible say about nature?
19

Question 8
Do you think extraterrestrial life is out there, and if so, what is its theological significance?
22

Question 9
Did Galileo start the war between science and religion?
25

Question 10
Does science disprove miracles?
28

Question 11
How can we understand Jesus in light of evolution?
31

Question 12
Do the two creation accounts in Genesis contradict each other?
34

Question 13
Aren't science and religion just two different things? Why not just let each one do their own thing and leave one another alone?
37

Question 14
Why do some people believe the earth is flat?
40

Question 15
As a Christian and a scientist, what do you think about atheism?
43

Question 16
What do you think about global warming?
46

Question 17
Are our beliefs about God just patterns of neurons firing in our brains and nothing more?
49

Question 18
What is the best academic class you ever took?
52

Question 19
What was the Star of Bethlehem?
55

Question 20
Were biblical years shorter than our current years?
58

Question 21
Why should people of good faith encourage scientific understanding?
61

Question 22
Doesn't it take faith to believe in science?
64

Question 23
Who is your favorite scientist?
67

Question 24
What do you mean by the expression that "wonder lies at the root of religion and science"?
70

Question 25
What is your favorite faith-and-science passage in the Bible?
73

Question 26
There is much in the Bible about heaven and earth, but isn't Mars cool too?
76

Question 27
Should Christians trust scientists?
79

Question 28
What is meant by the universe being "finely tuned" for the existence of life?
82

Question 29
How do faith and science come together for you in your daily practice of the Christian life?
85

Question 30
What is "intelligent design"?
88

Question 31
What is the multiverse, and what does it have to do with God?
91

Queston 32
If you invited your congregation into your classroom, what topic would you cover?
94

Question 33
Skepticism is important to the progress of science, but what role, if any, does skepticism play in the life of faith?
97

Question 34
If you could add one scientific idea into the language of the church, what would it be?
100

Question 35
If you leave this life, enter the pearly gates, and are allowed to ask God one scientific question, what would you ask?
103

Afterword
A conversation about reconciling faith and science
106

Introduction
All the way down and all the way out

Neil DeGrasse Tyson, an American astrophysicist and spokesman for science and reason, when asked in an interview if he believes in God responded:

> The more I look at the universe, the less convinced I am that there is something benevolent going on… I look at disasters that afflict Earth, and life on Earth: volcanoes, hurricanes, tornadoes, earthquakes, disease, pestilence, congenital birth defects. You look at this list of ways that life is made miserable on Earth by natural causes, and I just ask, "How do you deal with that?" I have no problems if, as we probe the origins of things, we bump into the Bearded Man. If that shows up, we good to go! Okay? Not a problem. There's just no evidence of it.[1]

Here Tyson is referring to what theologians call "natural evil," which is death and suffering caused by nonhuman agents. It's a time-worn problem and a pretty good argument against God.

Human beings do often suffer prolonged, brutal, and mindless ends. So, I get it when Tyson talks about nothing benevolent going on. There *are* all those diseases, after all, and natural disasters, and genetic mishaps. I'm surprised he didn't add a catastrophic asteroid impact to his list, which is simply a matter of time. But really, we don't need a list to know the truth: All lives, human and otherwise, are at every moment vulnerable to 10,000 oblivions.

Yet here I am, writing this introduction, and there you are, reading it. This fact is easily overlooked, but it is important. It took a lot of work to put this book together, and Good Faith Media and I have done our best. But you really have no idea. To make this book possible, you first must have a universe in which to have it. You need a bang—the bigger, the better. From the bang must come light, and from the light must come both matter and antimatter. But they must be a little off-balance so there's a bit more matter than antimatter: about 1,000,000,001 particles of matter for every 1,000,000,000 particles of antimatter. That's harder than it sounds.

Then you need to wait around for billions of years while nuclei are assembled inside stars and dying stars and supernovas. These nuclei must be bound together just right—not too loose, not too tight—and then they need to collect some stray electrons and drift around the cosmos for at least a few hundred million more years, settle down on a nice planet—not too hot, not too cold—and assemble themselves into molecules and then bacteria, which must, a billion years later, evolve into algae, then fish and amphibians and reptiles and weird rat-like primates and hominids and, finally, writers, publishers, and readers. The list of requirements and problems to solve is quite long, actually, before you ever get to things such as writing, marketing, and designing the cover.

But all this has actually happened, and here I am writing these words and there you are reading them. Here we are, communicating with one another in the midst of existence. I am impressed with existence, so much, in fact, that I believe Tyson's list of miseries, when weighed against the miracle of this moment, and against the cumulative miracle of all mornings and all evenings and all moments of existence, comes up short as an argument against God.

If it sounds strange to talk about existence, it is because existence is rarely acknowledged. It is rarely acknowledged because it is rarely sensed. Science can help us sense it, or art, music, sustained religious practice, great violence, or great loss can do it. But mostly we wander around "sunk into the everydayness of our own lives," in the words of Walker Percy.[2] In such a state it is easy to overlook the great generosity of existence.

Now existence is not only generous but also, by all reports and without exception, beautiful. By beautiful I do not mean pretty. Sister Wendy Beckett, a Roman Catholic nun and art critic, said it well: "Beauty is a not a pretty word, but it is a strong word."[3]

I know a man who might agree with Sister Wendy. In our family folklore he is known as Peter the Mean Neighbor. He lived near us years ago. He wasn't grumpy, and he wasn't cantankerous, and he wasn't depressed. He was *mean*. And he taught meanness to his son, who sometimes bullied my son Henry, two years younger than him. More than once I had to drive that young demon out of our yard, and more than once I had to explain to Henry that some people are just *mean*.

One summer afternoon a storm blew through and there appeared in the east a double rainbow the like of which I had never seen and have not seen since. I stood in our yard staring, stupefied.

Peter emerged from his house. His response was less reserved. A wide and wild smile broke across his lips. He whooped and hollered. His body sprang and twisted with each barbaric yawp. He looked like a bull rider without the bull. He was like a boy, new, vulnerable, not mean, filled to overflowing with this astonishing and holy thing. *This* is what beauty can do. Surely this was the work of God, a foretaste of the great and general feast.

"Now hold it right there," I hear Tyson say. Beauty, sure. But holiness? God? There is no evidence. But Tyson is a scientist, so he keeps an open mind. He says we still might "bump into the Bearded Man as we probe the origins of things." There's a little irony there, perhaps, but I want to know: What does Tyson *really* think it might look like if scientists were to bump into God?

In my own time as a scientist, I worked in two directions and ended up in two equally remote locations. As a graduate student and postdoctoral associate, I studied atomic nuclei. With our trusty proton accelerator, my colleagues and I drilled down into the heart of matter and mapped out details of certain nuclei, details no one had ever seen before. We were captained down the rabbit hole by quantum mechanics, a counterintuitive but reliable guide to the world of the impossibly tiny. And at no point on the journey did we bump into anything Tyson might recognize as divine. We found no bearded men, no encoded messages, no particles in the shape of Jesus, no stamp saying "Made by Yahweh," and my dissertation said nothing about God.

As an astrophysicist, I traveled in the other direction. Our group worked on quasars, among the most distant objects ever studied. I remember one quasar in particular: 3EG J2006-2321 (we astronomers really have a way with names). Its light traveled for seven *billion* years before being intercepted by our orbiting telescope. We collected and sifted data, and it was just as it had been in the nuclear lab: Not one of us bumped into God. And so, the paper on 3EG J2006-2321, just like every other paper in the *Astrophysical Journal*, is silent on the topic of God.

Drill deep into the heart of matter, and we do not bump into God. Peer outward to the edge of the big bang, and we do not find God. But what we do find is beauty, and plenty of it, all the way down and all the way out. Granted, this is not the obvious beauty of a double rainbow. It builds over time. It takes work. It fills the imagination with light and space and mathematics and existence. But does it fill us with God? With holiness?

I believe it does. Here I might leave Tyson and other empiricists and atheists behind, and that's fine; for all I know, they will enter the kingdom of God ahead of me. But the beauty of the world is not just epiphenomenal froth created by our oversized brains for the purpose of survival in a brutal cosmos. Scientific explanations are fine as far as they go, but sometimes they don't go far enough. Beauty, I say, is a reliable clue to the secret of the world. Beauty, I say, is recognition. It is the divine image in us recognizing itself in a world made, and being made, by God.

I think scientific study amplifies one's previous commitments. If Tyson brings mere skepticism to science, he will walk away more skeptical than ever. If I bring conventional religious belief to science, I will walk away slightly radicalized, knowing the cosmos is a cathedral and that God is not a code or a stamp, not a thing among things. God is instead the ground of all being, the mystery behind the beauty we call "existence." And science can only deepen that mystery; it does not and cannot solve it.

I hope this book increases your sense of wonder at the world while also adding a little to what you know about it. Some sentimental people believe that the more you know about the universe the less mysterious and wonderful it becomes, but knowledge and wonder do not compete; they cooperate. The more you learn about the cosmos, the more questions you have about it, the more conscious of your ignorance you become, and the more aware of wonder you become. This is the great paradox of learning.

Most religion-and-science dialogue suffers from peoples' overwhelming need, on virtually all sides of the discussion, to be right. This creates an atmosphere that repels those of us who love knowing things but who have also made peace with not knowing things, and with mystery. If this book alleviates this situation even a little, then I will be a happy and grateful author.

I thank Johnny Pierce and Bruce Gourley for taking me on as a regular columnist for *Nurturing Faith Journal*. They have been the finest of colleagues and the best of friends. I am also grateful for all others at Good Faith Media who have made my column and this book possible. And finally, I offer my largest thanks to you, my reader, and to all who have read my column, corresponded with me, and sent in questions. This book is dedicated to you.

Notes

[1] www.youtube.com/watch?v=I0nXG02tpDw.
[2] Walker Percy, *The Moviegoer* (Farrar, Strauss, and Giroux, 2019), 13.
[3] Image, *A Conversation with Sister Wendy Beckett*, vol. 27, 2003.

Question 1
Since you are a Baptist minister, are you a creationist?

I love science, I teach science, and I do science. I am also a pastor. I teach, I preach, and I attend to my congregation. I am one of many who hold science in one hand and faith in the other, who find no essential conflict between the two. I'm just more conspicuous about it than most people.

My colleague's question above reveals an assumption that many people hold about science and religion: that they are not only opposed, but essentially opposed. In his mind "Baptist minister" was synonymous with "creationist," and his confusion arose because he knew me as a member of the physics department faculty. How could I take both science and religion so seriously?

This popular idea of the opposition of science and religion has its origin in countless headlines, debates, online resources, and books that rely on and amplify the entertaining, easy-to-grasp idea of head-to-head conflict. Also the Galileo affair, the Scopes monkey trial, and other historical events are often regarded as evidence for a natural enmity between these two ways of knowing. So, there must be some truth to the idea that the religion-science relationship is primarily adversarial, right?

No, there really isn't any. The truth is: conflict sells. Conflict writes headlines, generates clicks, moves books, and makes for memorable stories. Only someone who took a course or did some research and reading on their own could discover the world of books, stories, videos, podcasts, and history celebrating and developing the rich dynamic relationship between science and the Christian faith. The truth is, a long spectrum of beliefs stretches out between the most strident creationist and the most rigid scientific atheist, and a hundred different viewpoints find a home on it.

Zoom into any point on the spectrum, to whatever resolution you like, and you will find nearly as many viewpoints on the spectrum as there are people who hold them. I will review eight of the major viewpoints below.

The first six fall under the heading of creationism, a variegated set of views held by those who insist that life arose from specific, identifiable acts of divine creation; who rely heavily on certain readings of the Bible to guide them in these efforts; and who reject scientific arguments that contradict their understanding of scripture. Unlike the final two, these six perspectives maintain, at least in part, some antagonism toward the methodology and conclusions of modern science. Here they are, in order of increasing emphasis on the role of science.

1. **Flat Earth**: Some people believe the earth is flat. Their belief is based largely upon ultraliteral readings of Genesis 1 and a deep conspiratorial suspicion of all nonbiblical authorities, including NASA; virtually all living people; elementary, middle, and high school teachers; and

Aristotle, who used a brilliant but simple scientific argument to prove, nearly 300 years before Jesus was born, that the earth is spherical. Many flat earth groups meet in bars and in homes, but over the last several years the Flat Earth International Conference has been held in Raleigh, Denver, and Dallas. Other public flat earth meetings have taken place in the United Kingdom, Italy, and Brazil.

2. **Geocentrism**: According to this belief, the earth is spherical and resides motionless in the center of the universe. Adherents of geocentrism tend to be very conservatve Christians. Perhaps the best-known geocentrist is Robert Sungenis, an American author and filmmaker who leads a Catholic splinter group known as Catholic Apologetics International and who in 2014 produced a full-length documentary, *The Principle*, to promote his geocentric viewpoint.

3. **Young Earth Creationism**: Here we have the most popular and best funded of all creationist perspectives. Ken Ham, with his organization Answers in Genesis, stands as the most famous advocate of this view, which admits a round earth and its motion around the sun but holds that the universe and everything in it was created about 6,000 years ago in six 24-hour periods, conforming to the Bible's literal timelines. Flat earthers and geocentrists tend to be young earth creationists also, but the majority of young earth creationists do not hold those more restrictive views.

4. **Gap Creationism**: Not all creationism is based on a young earth model. Gap creationism holds to the six literal days of creation found in Genesis 1 but posits a vast expanse of time between the first and second verses of Genesis, allowing for an old earth and consilience with a larger range of scientific theories than its young earth cousin. Oral Roberts and Jimmy Swaggart are two of the better-known names among gap creationists.

5. **Day-Age Creationism**: Perhaps the most popular version of old earth creationism, the day age theory suggests that the days of Genesis refer not to literal days, but can instead be lined up with certain epochs in cosmic history. It therefore relies on a metaphorical reading of English translations of Genesis while simultaneously keeping true to its overall timeline. The interpretation of the Hebrew word *yom*, which can be translated as both a 24-hour day and as an unspecified period of time, lies at the foundation of this perspective, as does 2 Pet. 3:8, which reads, "with the Lord one day is like a thousand years, and a thousand years are like one day." Many people hold this view, but Hugh Ross is perhaps its most well-known defender.

6. **Progressive Creationism**: This form of creationism accepts the general cosmic timeline suggested by scientists and microevolution (small, short-term changes within a species) but does not accept macroevolution (large, long-term changes including speciation). Advocates of this point of view believe that species do not appear gradually but are created fully formed in serial acts of divine creation at certain points in cosmic history. Sometimes this view overlaps with day age creationism.

The final two perspectives make room for a full acceptance of science, of its methods, and of its conclusions (which they understand to be ever and always tentative).

1. **Theistic Evolution**: This broad term comprises all views that find no essential conflict between Christian teaching on one hand, and the methodologies and conclusions of modern science on the other. This view is taught at most mainline Protestant seminaries and is the official view of the Roman Catholic Church.

2. **Atheistic Evolution**: This view fully accepts evolution and other scientific theories while rejecting the idea of God altogether. A connection is often (but not always) drawn between the two: If one accepts science, one cannot accept God. Like many extreme creationists, those who hold this perspective tend to think less about religion *and* science than they do religion *or* science. For them it is an either/or, and not a both/and, proposition. While the creationists come down on the side of religion, scientifically-motivated atheists come down on the side of science.

I myself adhere to theistic evolution, and write from that point of view. I love science; it is an intellectual adventure of the first order. The scientific enterprise is limited in scope and prone to error, but it is our best, most dependable means of addressing certain questions. In the long view it is self-correcting and tends toward reliability. Science, in my view, is one way to love God with all our minds. We have no reason to run from it or to defend our faith against it. As Galileo wrote more than 400 years ago, "I do not feel obliged to believe that the same God who endowed us with sense, reason, and intellect has intended us to forego their use."*

---

*See inters.org/galilei-madame-christina-Lorraine.

Question 2
How do you explain the Old Testament story of creation with your scientific methods?

The two Genesis accounts of creation were not written with modern science in mind, and scientific accounts of origins cannot be made to match up in any specific, chronological ways with biblical stories—not that people don't try. Some folks look to 2 Pet. 3:8, which says "with the Lord one day is like a thousand years, and a thousand years are like one day" to warrant their claim that the six days of creation match up with six particular periods of cosmic history. In this view God's words "Let there be light" (Gen. 1:3) correspond to the flood of photons that emanated from the big bang 13.8 billion years ago, the separation of the earth from the waters (Gen. 1:9) corresponds to the formation of the planet 4.5 billion years ago, and so on.

Other folks go further. They appeal to Einstein's theory of relativity, which tells us that time is relative.* This means, for example, that six days from one perspective (or "frame of reference") is equivalent to billions of years in another. This is true. Time *is* relative and does not flow at the same pace for all people at all times. This effect is not obvious to us in our daily lives. But if we routinely zipped around at speeds close to that of light—or if the speed of light were much less than it is—this strange flexibility of time would seem commonplace. And it is, in fact, possible to find two frames of reference such that a certain set of events lasts six days in one and 13.8 billion years in another.

But just because it's possible to look at the Bible through the lens of relativity doesn't mean it's a good idea. This kind of thinking places a strange and uniquely modern strain on scripture. By forcing ancient texts to fit into the categories of contemporary science, it distorts them beyond their breaking point. The text becomes a code to be cracked rather than a living document. The real point of the Genesis stories is theological and relational: they tell us how God, human beings, and the cosmos are interrelated. They tell us who we are and what the cosmos is in the context of divine creativity and love. And they do so by using the primary medium of the age: prose and poetry, not the abstractions of modern physical science.

It's unwise to apply specific scientific theories to the interpretation of scripture, yet I find resonances between the Old Testament and scientific accounts of creation. For starters, Genesis actually encourages the practice of science. Ancient Israel, unlike other ancient civilizations, considered the world to be neither divine nor corrupt. To the west, the Egyptians thought the sun and the moon and the soil and the Nile River (among other parts of the natural world) manifested aspects of

---

*See, for example, Gerald Schroeder, *Genesis and the Big Bang* (Bantam, 1991).

gods and goddesses; these parts of creation were themselves sacred. To the east, the Babylonians viewed the material world as essentially corrupt; their creation account said that the earth and sky were constructed from two halves of a goddess' ruptured corpse and that human beings were made to be slaves of the gods.

Israel took a middle way. Genesis describes the cosmos as a thing of great goodness and integrity but not itself sacred: the sun and moon are lights, not gods. Also, creation is not intrinsically debased: the heavens and earth were produced not through violence but through a series of ordered and deliberate divine words. Also, for ancient Israel as for us, human beings were viewed as free and worthy creations, not slaves of God or gods. According to Genesis, matter is valuable and worth studying in its own right because it's pronounced good by God. And because it is not divine, we are free to study it on its own terms. We who have inherited Israel's creation story are free to do science! But there's more.

The Bible describes the cosmos as having the capacity to generate life. It is integrated and robust, just as biology tells us. I cannot help but hear overtones of evolution in God's command for the sea to "bring forth swarms of living creatures" and for the earth to "bring forth living things of every kind" (Gen. 1:20, 24). I don't mean that the authors of Genesis foresaw evolution in any meaningful way. But the writer(s) must have observed just how vigorous and sturdy and life-producing the world is, and how creation itself holds the potential—drawn out and realized through the divine word—to create.

Genesis is not the only book in the Old Testament that addresses creation. This is a point often missed in discussions of science and scripture. Distinct perspectives on the cosmos may be found in Psalms, Isaiah, Ecclesiastes, and other books.

Perhaps the strangest such perspective is found in the book of Job. When the character Job is beaten down by a series of terrible losses despite his morally unimpeachable life, he pleads to God for justice, and God eventually responds with the longest divine speech in the Bible.

In this speech God does not explain or defend Job's suffering, nor does the Lord offer an apology. Instead, God takes Job on a most unexpected tour of the cosmos, a hard ride through the cosmic outlands. In one of the most unusual passages in the Bible, God sweeps Job up off the ash heap upon which he mourns, draws him down to the roots of the earth, shows him the expanse of the sea and the fountains of the deep, and catapults him through the constellations. But this is just the beginning. Job is treated next to a series of close looks at individual wild animals. Almost without exception these creatures inhabit the barren and dangerous wilderness at the periphery of Job's world: the mountain goat, the wild ass, the ostrich, and the vulture are central exhibits. Finally, God brings Job face-to-face with Behemoth and Leviathan, mythic and terrifying creatures that represent cosmic chaos.

Goats and ostriches do not seem cosmic to us. In Atlanta, where I live, we have these animals in the zoo, some in the petting zoo even, along with vultures and other creatures mentioned in Job. But for Job these beasts were marginal, never thought about, gamey and embarrassing and bloody dots on the outer fringe of his consciousness. But in the light of God's tour, they are seen to be beautiful and free creatures living in their own communities, communities from which human civilization itself appears peripheral and unimportant. God, it turns out, loves more than us human beings.

In Job's cosmos we are the marginal ones. Job therefore has much in common with contemporary scientific views of the universe in which we seem to be an afterthought at best: We are recent additions to a vast and ancient and evolving cosmos that has no center and no edges, that favors no planet and no star and no galaxy, that has a remote and violent past and is expanding ever more rapidly into an uncertain future. If the book of Job were written today, God would show Job all of this: evolution both cosmic and biological, the disorienting scale of things, and maybe even extraterrestrial life.

The Old Testament contains other takes on creation. Psalm 104 celebrates the same cosmos as Job but from the perspective of joy and not loss. The author of Ecclesiastes, ever the cynic, casts the cosmos as cyclical and pointless. Isaiah 40–45 imagines a new creation to accompany the end of exile and the return of Israel to their homeland.

The relation between biblical creation and the cosmos as we know it today is not simply a matter of finding scientific concepts buried like so many secrets in the text of the Bible. It is much deeper and broader—and much more interesting—than that!

Question 3
How were you able to study science in school and allow room for your faith to grow?

I was 9 years old when I first sensed a conflict between faith and science. It didn't start in school or at church. It started at home. And I know I was 9 because it happened on Nov. 7, 1977. That is the date on the cover of a certain issue of *Time* magazine. It is also the date when, for me, evolution got personal.

The magazine appeared in our mailbox and ended up in my hands. On the cover was a fellow named Richard Leakey kneeling beside what was to me a hideous-looking creature. It was apelike but also vaguely human in appearance. It had a giant head, broad high cheekbones, strangely long arms, and small dark beady eyes looking straight at the camera. It was a model of *Homo habilis*, a species that lived in East Africa several million years ago. Above the picture were the words, "How Man Became Man."

I sat down with the magazine, and I figured it out pretty quickly. Mr. Leakey and *Time* were telling me that this brute was my ancestor. Today the connection between *Homo habilis* and *Homo sapiens* has been cast into doubt, but the details of the science do not matter. All that mattered is, I was horrified to think that human beings—me, my family, my friends, all of us—were related to any such creature. It bothered me that Mr. Leakey seemed to be fine with this. He seemed like a nice guy. It seemed wrong and made me sad. The whole thing hurt my feelings.

The problem grew worse when, a year or so later, Dad showed me a geologic timeline in a natural history book. It presented, in detail, the scientific story of life on Earth. A vast host of weird extinct animals appeared in the timeline, but Adam and Eve did not. Their absence was conspicuous. Meanwhile, my Bible was silent on extinctions, trilobites, and *T. rex*. The whole thing shook me up and filled me with a strange and vast wonder.

During high school, faith and science lived in an uneasy tension inside of me. I couldn't really see how the two fit together, but I never seriously questioned science. Science was always delivered to me—by my dad, who was himself a scientist, and by my teachers—in such a calm, direct way that it never once struck me as unbelievable. It was always religion, which seemed so emotionally driven, that lost ground. And by the time I reached college and began studying physics, my faith had simply faded away. I wasn't angry: Christianity just seemed, on balance, unlikely and insufficient and irrational in the light of the cosmos I was learning about. So, I just dropped it.

But later I picked it up again, and I didn't have to let go of science to do so. In fact, I returned to faith while I was working on my PhD in physics; there was never a question of compromising science. I just began to understand religion, faith, and the Bible differently. If I had to choose a single word to describe this change, it would be *enlargement*. The rather conventional Protestantism with which I grew up, like so many local expressions of faith, was limited from an intellectual point of view. Historically, culturally, and theologically, my church upbringing was narrow. I loved the church of my youth, and I was truly loved by people there. But as I entered adulthood, I needed more. I needed a larger faith.

And over time I got it. I can't say how exactly, but my years in a Catholic high school might have laid some of the groundwork. I began to see that Christianity is a far larger, more complex and diverse and interesting tradition than I had ever known. In particular, I saw beyond the clichés about the conflict between science and religion. With God's help, I began to rebuild a faith that works.

My change in perspective can be explained in terms of two simple Venn diagrams. In my earlier view, Christianity and science basically stood apart from one another and had equal standing. While I was in high school and college, I viewed Christianity and science as competing ways of knowing. In my mind, each had no real need of the other and it was not possible to stand in any place that was covered by both. It was one or the other, either/or. So, there was conflict.

In my current view, Christianity and science are not opposed. I see science as contained within Christianity. Conflict arises only when you remove science from its context and try to set it up as its own, independent worldview. Science is not sufficient to stand on its own in this way. There are too many normal human questions—about meaning, value, and purpose—that science simply does not address. The facts and theories of science need a context: for me, Christianity provides that context. But my faith needed to be enlarged for this to occur. It had to grow in order to contain science. That's what happened as I entered adulthood.

You may ask: How did I leave room for my faith to grow? How did I get to where my faith could grow large enough to encompass science and the cosmos it has shown us? My answer, and it may seem paradoxical, is this: I dropped it. I let my faith go.

Let's rewind to my later high school years. That was when I began to sense my faith constricting around me. It did not help with questions I had about life, including scientific questions, because its answers suddenly seemed small and irrational and beside the point. As a senior, I played the role of pastor on Youth Sunday at church. I don't recall what I said in the pulpit that day, but I do remember the uncomfortable feeling of selling something I didn't believe in. I felt disconnected from the faith that at one time comforted, inspired, and challenged me.

But what I felt wasn't my faith constricting; it was me growing. I was beginning to leave behind a faith that no longer worked. It was starting to pinch and chafe and to do little else. So, within a few months, after moving away from home for the first time, I no longer went to church, no longer prayed, and simply dropped the tradition of my youth. Why should I keep holding onto something that served no good purpose?

The language is important: I didn't push my faith away. I just let it go because it did not seem to square with what I was learning about the world, including science. I never became an atheist, militant or otherwise. And I suppose it's because my mind and heart never turned against God in any rigid or absolute way that I was able to return to Christianity after a number of years away.

For me it was essential to let the beliefs of my childhood go in order to discover a faith that worked in adult life and in the world of science. Once this happened, my faith began to expand, and today it is roomy enough for science, trilobites, *T. rex*, *Homo habilis*, and the whole wild and woolly cosmos we call home.

Question 4
Why do scientists think their calculations for the age of the universe (almost 13.8 billion years) and the size of the universe (billions and billions of light-years) are better than beliefs based on the Bible?

Suppose your child tells you he feels bad. You place your hand on his forehead: it feels hot. You break out an oral thermometer: after a minute it reads 102.2°F. Just to be sure, you try a fancy in-ear device: it reads 102.0.

Does your boy have a fever? Yes. Three independent measurements tell you so. They are not equally reliable and the numbers you get are somewhat different, but there's no way all three measurements are wrong, and in the *exact* same way. You can say with all confidence that his temperature is in the neighborhood of 102. It might be 101.9, and it might be 102.3. You can't say for sure, but it doesn't matter because you know what you need to know: It's time to call the doctor.

We think the universe is about 13.8 billion years old. Like the 102° fever, this figure is derived from a number of different measurements. Three of these are:

- observations of stars called "white dwarfs"
- something called the "cosmic microwave background"
- the recession velocities of distant galaxies

Each of these methods, taken separately, point to an age in the neighborhood of 13.8 billion years. If the age of the cosmos were significantly different than this, then these methods—and others I have not mentioned—must not only be wrong individually, but also wrong in such a way that they give the same answer.

This is not possible. As with the hand, the oral thermometer, and the in-ear device, these methods are independent. They do not depend on the same assumptions or principles, so the probability of them all giving the same wrong answer is zero. Also, just as in the measurement of the child's temperature, different methods produce slightly different ages. The universe might be 13.7 billion years old according to one method, and it might be 13.9 billion according to another, but we know what we need to know: The cosmos is about 13.8 billion years old.

This contradicts a plain reading of scripture. If you take the Bible and simply count back the years from the time of Jesus, you will find that creation week occurred about 6,000 years ago. Many people believe this is an accurate date for the origin of the universe.

A different (and much larger) group of independent observations do not indicate that the cosmos is 13.8 billion years old, but they *do* tell us it is more than 6,000. Three of these observations are the distances of nearby stars, radioactivity in the earth's crust, and plate tectonics. Again, these methods independently point to the same conclusion: The earth and the cosmos have been around much longer than 6,000 years.

You ask about the size of the universe. Its size is related to its age. The cosmos has been expanding for the last 13.8 billion years, and today it spans many billions of light-years. A host of overlapping methods determines the distances to stars and galaxies, and together these methods form something astronomers call the "distance ladder." The lowest rungs on the ladder are used for our nearest neighbors. For example, the distances to the closest stars are measured by *parallax* (our eyes and brain use parallax to produce depth perception for nearby objects). More distant objects require other methods, which themselves depend on parallax. Some of these methods are more dependable than others, but refinements in observing methods and constant cross-checking result in the increasing reliability of the distance ladder.

All of this work rests upon certain assumptions. For example, we assume that the speed of light does not change, so that it was the same billions of years ago as it is today. We also assume that rates of radioactivity have not changed and that the physics that applies out in space is no different than the physics that applies here on Earth. Scientists are aware of these and other assumptions and are always testing them.

Another reason we trust our assumptions is, they have led us to a largely self-consistent understanding of the cosmos. For a simple example of this, the age of the earth is less than the age of the universe, even though the ages of both are determined in completely different ways. Also, the age of the universe is greater, but not much greater, than the age of the oldest stars. And the time required for stars to produce the elements needed for life is far less than the age of the universe. The list is long.

Pieces of the puzzle remain missing. Major questions are still being asked. This is to be expected—it has always been so. But the sense one gets from looking at the scientific work of the last five centuries is that of overall consistency and fruitfulness. This would be quite surprising if our assumptions were all wrong.

A simple argument remains available to anyone who disagrees with the scientific consensus: Perhaps God engineered the cosmos to appear much older than it is. Maybe God created the cosmos to look for all the world as if it is billions of light-years across. Maybe light from distant stars and galaxies was created in mid-flight. Maybe South America and Africa were formed to look exactly as if they were part of a single original continent and have been drifting apart for 200,000,000 years. Maybe the cosmic microwave background radiation, which scientists believe is a relic of the big bang, was put in place to make it appear as if the cosmos was 13.8 billion years old.

This is of course deeply problematic. What would be the sense of God minutely adjusting the cosmos to appear in every detail to be 13.8 billion years old? To test our faith?

Any God who would manipulate the universe in such a way—just to test us—is not a God we can trust. That God would be an anti-rational agent of disorder. That God would be rooting for us to reject our own God-given capacities for reason, imagination, and creativity. That God would be a deceiver. That God would contradict scripture in ways that really matter. And that God is not the God of life and love and reason and wonder in whom we all believe.

Question 5
Taking into account scientific calculations for the size and expansion and age of the cosmos, what is your view of the spiritual significance of humans in the universe?

Imagine standing in a rowboat in the middle of the Pacific Ocean, looking through a telescope at the horizon. No matter how good your telescope is, you can see no further than a few miles. This is because the earth is spherical and the ocean curves down and away from you in every direction. Three miles in every direction: that's all you'll ever get. The geometry of the problem is nonnegotiable. The horizon is the limit of what you can see, but because you know about the shape of the planet, you're also aware there's a whole lot more you can't see.

This provides a nice analogy for us earthlings looking out into space. Our cosmic horizon lies a little further away, about 40 billion light-years away in every direction. (A light year is the distance light travels in a year, about 6 trillion miles. It is not a measure of time.) Within that distance there are approximately a hundred billion galaxies, each containing billions of stars and planets. But just as the great majority of the Pacific Ocean lies outside the three-mile limit as seen from the rowboat, most of the cosmos is permanently out of reach of not only our best present technology, but also of any technology whatsoever.

To say that the earth is a drop in the ocean of space is so frantically understated as to be laughable. We would need to compare a single drop of water to 1,000,000,000,000,000,000,000,000 Pacific oceans to begin to get a decent comparison. And this is only the space within our horizon. It is cozy compared to what lies beyond, untold light-years' worth of galaxies and stars and planets that in principle we cannot ever see or know about. What kind of life is thriving out there, both within and beyond our cosmic horizon?

A similarly dizzying picture can be drawn with respect to time. Imagine compressing all of cosmic history into a single year, so that the big bang happened on January 1 at 12:00 a.m. and right now is the ringing-out of the year on midnight of December 31. The year contains 31,500,000 seconds, and recorded human history—since the invention of writing by the Sumerians 5,300 years ago—spans only 12 of them. We are newcomers, to say the least!

We are also one of millions of related species, billions if we consider the whole history of life. We share lineage not only with chimpanzees and gorillas, but also with whales and okapis and lichen and oak trees. All life is related. (And, don't forget, there may be a lot more life than we can imagine out among the stars.) How then are we significant? How then are we special?

Let's consider three possible responses. First, we could say that human beings are not special at all. Physical insignificance and spiritual insignificance go together in this view. Since we are unimaginably tiny and brand new compared to the cosmos, and since we occupy no special location in the universe, and since there are all these other species to which we are genetically related, and since our ancestors were not human, then we must be mere organisms similar to all the others and that's all there is to it. In this view all life is basically the same and is physically and spiritually insignificant.

This view is obviously contrary to Christianity, for it has the effect of removing the word "spirit" from our language altogether. All life is devalued here, and if life is not spiritually significant, nothing is. So, this is not an option.

Second, we could say that none of these facts of science matter, that there is no relationship between the physical and the spiritual. We can be the most significant of creatures in God's eyes even if we are incomprehensibly tiny, newly arrived, surrounded by intimately related species and possibly by a whole cosmos full of extraterrestrial life. Our unique spiritual souls and the life to come are all that really matter, not this present world. From a truly spiritual point of view, it would make no difference if the cosmos were much smaller and younger, if we were not related to other life, and if there were no possibility of there being intelligent creatures out there among the galaxies. The details of the cosmos simply do not matter.

This view is also unsatisfying. Christianity, more than almost any other major religion, insists that the physical and the spiritual are not opposed but are instead deeply related. God created all things and called them very good. We believe that the divine nature is somehow revealed in the cosmos; therefore, the material and physical worlds cannot be separated. This principle finds its ultimate expression in the incarnation of God in the flesh and blood of Jesus of Nazareth. At the very least we, as followers of that same Jesus, cannot simply disregard facts about the material cosmos. These facts have something important to tell us.

But what do they tell us? We turn again to the Old Testament book of Job, which offers a clue to a third way of looking at this question. In that story Job is a wise judge and a generous advocate of the poor and needy. He sits atop the social pyramid. In his world this means that not only his fellow man but also God favors him—his material and social status is a sign of his righteousness before God. There is no question about it: Job is significant.

As the story unfolds, Job loses his family, his health, and his wealth. But, importantly for us, he loses something else: his significance. He finds himself on the outside, no longer important to anyone. He no longer occupies a seat of judgment and power. He longs for the significance he once had, and wonders why it was taken from him. Is it possible that he is truly insignificant, even in God's eyes?

After many chapters of arguing about this with his friends, God speaks to Job. But God does not explain Job's loss of significance. Instead, God points Job toward creation. Job is taken on a tour of the cosmos. First, he gets an eyeful of the earth and the sea and the stars. He is then shown an array of strange animals, creatures that occupy the outer fringes of his consciousness and of his human world, thriving in places where he could never survive. These beasts have no connection with Job's world of commerce, religion, and justice. They do not value what Job values. God shows Job that the mountain goat, the wild ass, the ostrich, the wild ox, the vulture, and many other animals form communities of their own, communities from which Job's own world looks small and peripheral.

During the tour, God points out repeatedly how these animals are divinely cared for. The eye of God is on all of creation, not just the tiny piece of it that concerns Job. God is not preoccupied with human beings; instead, God's providence balances the needs of all creatures, meeting each one at its own level. God knows every part of creation and is fully present to all things. There is not a star or a stone or a fish or a bird that God does not sustain. The love of God is sufficient for the whole cosmos, including the deer, the lion, and the eagle.

It is also sufficient for Job. In the end, Job is satisfied with God's answer. He is set free to no longer worry about his own significance, because he has experienced the love of God. So it goes for us. In the face of such cosmic love, we are not only free to forget about our own importance but also are set free to love one another, all creatures. And above all, whatever Job thought of himself, God thought enough of Job to show up for him when he called from the ash heap.

Question 6
How have you furthered your faith through your work as a scientist?

In Genesis we read that God created all things and called them very good. An artist and a work of art provide a common metaphor for this foundational Christian belief: just as an artist's thoughts and personality are revealed in a painting or a song or a poem, the cosmos reveals something of the (very good) divine nature.

This is helpful as far as it goes, but I find that it doesn't go far enough. When a human being creates a work of art and walks away from it, the meaning or significance of the painting is not affected. This is because the creation is external to its human creator and, although it continues to reveal something of the artist, the work is not diminished by the artist's absence. The problem is that the artist is fully external to the creation, and I don't believe God is fully external to the cosmos. Instead, we and the cosmos "live and move and have our being" *in* God (Acts 17:28).

I think of all the cosmos—celestial, terrestrial, biological—as a great window, a window marked with color and life and sound and motion. God made this window in order to shine through it. If God walks away from it, the creation may still exist in some form, but it goes dark. The colors fade, life stagnates, and beauty vanishes. That is, creation loses its vitality and meaning. (In this way the cosmos functions somewhat akin to an icon.)

As a scientist, I explore the window. My job is to find new sections and panels and colors. The window of creation is an infinite and variegated and ever-changing thing, and exploring it has kept many people busy for thousands of years. There is no end to the wonder of this exploration.

My work in science has drawn me closer to God because exploring the window allows me to see the light more clearly, or to see it in new patterns, or new colors, or new details. That is, exploring the window is learning about both the window and the light. To explore the window is to learn about both the window *and* the light.

It is a thrilling to glimpse light passing through a thin slice of the window no one has ever seen before. This has happened to me twice.

My first glimpse occurred deep within a particular atomic nucleus we call phosphorus-30. Such a nucleus is a tiny buzzing jumble of protons and neutrons—15 of each—and sits at the center of a phosphorous atom the way the sun sits at the center of the solar system. An atom itself is a vanishingly small speck, so the nucleus is tiny beyond comprehension.

But the protons and neutrons we call phosphorus-30 do not swirl about at random; they run along a set of fixed paths, and there are many ways to arrange them on these paths. ("Paths" is a manner of speaking here, not a scientific concept.) What I found, as a graduate student, was a new way of arranging the protons and neutrons on their pathways within phosphorus-30.

This discovery merited a congratulatory smile from my advisor and a few sentences in a single journal article 20 years ago. Nothing has been said about it since. It was a modest discovery, and I knew it. But I was elated. It was my first time to unearth a brand-new fact, to see a tiny slice of the cosmos unseen by anyone in all history. That it was "out of the way" and utterly peripheral to everyone else on the planet mattered not at all. I had experienced what Richard Feynman called "the pleasure of finding things out," and what I might call "the joy of seeing the light."

My second glimpse was a bigger deal and had to do with the peculiar nature of a galaxy called 3EG J2006-2321. This thing is as big as atoms are small, and as remote as atoms are near. It resides some 10 billion light-years away and is probably about 100,000 light-years across (a light year is the distance light travels in a year, about 6 trillion miles). It is a gamma-ray blazar, an unusual beast, a galaxy caught in its earliest stages of formation. More of these galaxies have been discovered since, but at the time it was important enough to merit a full journal article.

Like my phosphorus-30 discovery, my identification of 3EG J2006–2321 did not make headlines or upend any established scientific theories. But in both cases I was thrilled by the sense of having learned something no one had ever known. They were for me small but undeniable glimpses into what Stephen Hawking was fond of calling the "mind of God."

Between these nuclear and galactic extremes, the cosmos stretches out in my imagination. As a scientist and professor, I have had the opportunity to study and teach about some of it, and my understanding of the cosmos, limited though it is, has had a profound effect on my faith. It has deepened my wonder and my gratitude for life.

Some of my happiest glimpses through the window of creation have not come while working in an official scientific capacity. They did not happen near the extreme ends of the scale. They have not been about physics or astronomy. They were not even discoveries in the full sense of the word. That is, these findings were new to me but not to humanity. Mostly they had to do with birds.

I could tell many bird stories at this point, but it suffices to say that birds are my constant companions. Every species has its own way of being in the world, and even individual birds have their quirks. Familiar ones attend daily to the feeders in my yard. I live near a large creek, and I visit it as often as possible. I take my binoculars and my field guide. Down there I know where the red-tailed hawk keeps its nest, when to expect the pileated woodpeckers to show up, and how the ruby-crowned kinglets join forces with the Carolina chickadees when they forage. I see new species during the fall and spring migration seasons. Even quick trips to the creek make me happy. Every time, without fail, I learn something new.

I am not an expert on birds. At my level it is easy and fun to learn new things about them. Such glimpses through the window are open to everyone; you don't need to be a scientist to fall in love with creation and to see God shine through it.

Not that being a scientist doesn't make a difference. The most powerful lesson I have learned from science, and there may be no other way to learn it in the way I'm talking about, is that we are profoundly ignorant. The world is not finite. We have no complete knowledge of anything. In science as in life, we see through a glass darkly. No window is perfectly transparent.

And no explanation is ever complete. This is definitely true in science. Every theory, no matter how successful, multiplies questions while pushing them deeper. The cosmos is not self-explanatory. We know next to nothing about reality. Internalizing this fact leads to what I call "feelings of a small self," that is, humility—a virtue we as Christians are called to embrace time and again.

Question 7
What does the Bible say about nature?

For us 21st-century people, the words "nature" and "natural" stand in distinction to the word "supernatural" and everything suggested by it: the spiritual, the nonmaterial, the divine, God, miracles. A common view, which has been shaped largely by the Enlightenment, says that nature runs according to set laws that might or might not be suspended now and again by a divine hand. Many people who believe in God say such suspensions make room for miracles, whereas many atheists say they never happen at all.

Both views, however, are foreign to scripture, because the Bible does not recognize any distinction between the natural and the supernatural. Its understanding of the world is not ours. It says nothing about what we today call nature. It instead talks about creation, which stresses not the world set apart from God—as does the language of natural and supernatural—but the relation between the world and God. After all, there is no creation without a creator.

This is not to say that the Bible is silent about the sea or stars or animals or trees: it talks about these things often. But it always understands them to be intimately connected to God. It refers to them always in a theological context and with the assumption, stated up front in Genesis 1, that each and every created thing is a good expression of the divine character. It is precisely their rootedness in God that makes them good.

In other words, from the Bible's point of view we may hope to learn something of God by looking to creation. When the Bible mentions creation, it is by extension talking about the divine character. And it mentions creation a lot.

But not everything it says about creation squares up neatly and consistently. Within scripture many perspectives on creation combine in ways that seem to fill out a rich and complex personality. Four pairs of contrasting traits mix to form a kind of biblical character sketch of creation.

First, creation is stable yet creative. The integrity of creation is made evident throughout the Old Testament. In the opening pages of Genesis, we find a cosmos that is grounded in God's will, while 1 Chron. 16:30 is just one of several passages claiming that "the world is firmly established; it shall never be moved." While some commentators have understood this to mean that the earth is not in motion, the larger point is that we can trust the ground beneath our feet just as we can trust God. That is, both creation and the Creator are reliable, rational, and prone to consistency.

Yet the world is given real agency by God and is itself deeply creative—a creative creation! In Gen. 1:20 and 1:24 we find God commanding the earth and the sea to bring forth swarms of living creatures. God does not create these fish and animals directly but is assisted by the elements themselves. We may conclude that God endowed creation with an ability to produce and sustain life. Meanwhile, Prov. 8:22-31 describes the created order as a boundless playground well suited to wisdom's creative imagination and love for the world. From the biblical point of view, this combination of stability and inventiveness is an important mark of creation.

Second, creation is promise-filled yet already jubilant. Scripture often refers to creation with a future orientation. In Isaiah the earth holds the promise of redemption; the prophet uses a renewed creation as a symbol of Israel's restoration. "I will make the wilderness a pool of water, and the dry land springs of water," the Lord promises in 41:18. In chapter 11, Isaiah speaks to Israel of a future in which the wolf will lie down with the lamb and creation will be restored "in all my holy mountain." And in Romans 8, Paul writes of creation as being in travail as a woman giving birth, groaning for future deliverance and adoption.

But joy already has a hold on the earth. This is true not only in the wisdom passage of Proverbs 8 but also in the book of Psalms, and especially in Psalm 104. This song rejoices in all of creation, from the stars above to the birds in their nests to the great sea monster Leviathan. It revels in grass, trees, rain, and in creation's bounty: oil, wine, bread. So, the joy of creation is therefore both *already* and *not yet*.

Third, creation is benign yet unsafe. For much of the biblical narrative, creation acts as a kind of colorful backcloth, an ever-present symbol of God's goodness, power, and providence. Elijah is sustained by birds in the wilderness (1 Kgs. 17:6), Job is healed by a cosmic vision (Job 38–41), and Amos draws on images of creation to describe God's treatment of the wounds of injustice (Amos 5:24).

Yet creation threatens, particularly at the periphery. In the wilderness we find uncertainty and danger, both on land and at sea. Chaos rages at the margins of creation. Yet God loves these places and their creatures (Job 39–41). The world, called "good" by God, is nowhere called domesticated and safe. At times it even turns hostile; the great sea monster Leviathan, clearly one of God's creations, is described as a force to be overcome (see Psalm 74 and Isaiah 27).

The known and unknown meet in the wilderness, a liminal place where an unsafe and mysterious God might be encountered. The margins of creation are places of purification, an always-frightening experience. We find many examples of this in scripture, including:

- Jacob wrestling with God (Gen. 32:22-32)
- Moses and the burning bush (Exod. 3:1-5)
- The delivery of the law at Sinai (Exod. 19:20-25)
- The wandering of the Israelites (Exodus 14 and following)
- John the Baptist (Mark 1:4-8)
- Jesus tempted in the desert (Luke 4:1-13)

Creation heals but it also threatens.

Fourth, creation is personalized yet indifferent. In Genesis 2 a garden is created by God especially for us—custom-made for humanity. Meanwhile, the Lord spreads out the heavens similar to a tent (see Ps. 104:2, Isa. 40:22, Jer. 10:12). This image is an indication of the habitability of the earth and is a powerful symbol of the comforts and protections of home.

But in Ecclesiastes things take a dark turn: creation exhibits a supreme indifference to human needs. The cycles of days, seasons, years, and lifetimes come and go without end and without significance. For the author of Ecclesiastes, creation seems pointless. In direct contradiction to much of the Bible, it is described as renewing nothing, producing little, and ceaselessly turning back on itself in a series of closed and decaying loops. "Vanity of vanities! All is vanity! The sun rises and the sun goes down, and hurries to the place where it rises. The wind blows to the south, and goes round to the north… all streams run to the sea, but the sea is not full… all things are wearisome; more than one can express" (from Ecclesiastes 1). Similar sentiments are expressed in 12:1-8. Another complexity is added to the mix: the Bible views the created order as both made for human beings but also aloof to our unending search for meaning.

Overall, then, scripture develops a view of creation that seems more like a personality sketch than a scientific treatise, which tracks nicely with the first thesis of Western religion. The fundamental reality we call God is more like a who than a what, more like a person than a thing. It stands to reason that the creation would reflect the supremely personal nature of this God.

Question 8
Do you think extraterrestrial life is out there, and if so, what is its theological significance?

The Christian tradition says nothing about extraterrestrial life. But our faith does tell us about God, and one of God's attributes is creativity. When it comes to life, God invents endlessly.

Genesis 1–3, Psalm 104, Job 38–41, and other scripture passages describe the works of an innovative, imaginative, ingenious, and indefatigable Creator. The author of Genesis is clear about the deliberate care God takes with the fish of the sea and beasts of the land. The psalmist overflows with praise in the presence of God's creations: the lion, the hyrax, the cedar, the stork. Job is taken on a cosmic tour during which God praises the deer, the eagle, the vulture, and the mountain goat, among other odd and remote creatures. Throughout scripture the living world provides evidence of God's creative nature.

Today we know more about the earth's biodiversity than we did when the Bible was written. Even though there is much more for us to learn, we are sure of this: Life is everywhere it can be. It thrives in the deepest trenches of the oceans, on the highest mountaintops, and at the outer extremes of temperature and humidity. In 2013, scientists reported that bacteria were found living a half-mile under the Antarctic ice. Life has also been found thousands of feet below the ocean floor, itself many thousands of feet deep, off the northwestern coast of the United States.

The lives of some creatures evoke true wonder. Tiny animals called tardigrades can withstand temperatures from −458°F to +300°F, radiation hundreds of times more intense than the lethal dose for humans, and the vacuum of outer space. And there's more: According to Wikipedia, "[Tardigrades] can go without food or water for more than 30 years, drying out to the point where they are 3% or less water, only to rehydrate, forage, and reproduce." They prefer to live on moss and lichen but can be found nearly everywhere, from the peaks of mountains to the floor of the sea, in deserts, in rainforests, on volcanoes, in Antarctica.

Tardigrades provide just one example. Earth is wholly saturated with life. It contains 10,000 bird species; 6,000 red algae species; 15,000 moss species; and at least 1,000,000 insect species. The list goes on. Life shows up and persists and diversifies everywhere it can. This divine creativity, praised in scripture and revealed in the world around us, overflows in gratuitous, generous, extravagant ways everywhere we look.

It seems that, given the endless forms of life with which God has blessed and filled every corner and fold of our home planet, the same rule might apply to the cosmos itself: Out among the stars, perhaps life is everywhere it *can* be. Perhaps God's creativity demands it.

The question remains, however: Is life really out there? Scientists have been working on this question for decades. For many years this work was largely a hunt for radio communications from outer space, but recently it has focused on finding planets orbiting stars other than the sun. Today, thanks to the success of this effort, the search for extraterrestrial life has entered a kind of golden age.

When I first took astronomy in 1987, we knew of no planets outside our solar system, and by the time I started teaching the subject in 1997 we knew of only three such planets. Many more of these bodies, known as extrasolar planets or exoplanets, have been discovered in the decades since. As of Oct. 21, 2022, there are 5,190 confirmed exoplanets and 8,954 exoplanet candidates.* The study of these planets will almost certainly provide clues about the origin, evolution, and fate of our own planet and solar system. But the true driver behind exoplanet research is the question: Are we alone?

Exoplanets help us answer this question because not even tardigrades can live long, full lives on a star or in outer space. Life as we know it requires liquid water, which can only exist in regions close to stars (so the water won't freeze) but not too close (so the water won't vaporize). Planets such as the earth, where water can exist as a liquid, are, we believe, the best—and perhaps the only—possible candidate locations for life. Hence the great interest in studying exoplanets.

All of these thousands of exoplanets and exoplanet candidates lie close at hand, at least when measured on the scale of the Milky Way, our home galaxy. Current technology simply can't detect planets beyond our stellar neighborhood. But if we assume that our neighborhood is not unusually rich in planets, and we have no reason to believe that it is, there must be at least 100 billion planets in the Milky Way alone. (And the Milky Way is only one of hundreds of billions of galaxies in the visible universe.) With such an incomprehensibly vast number of planets to choose from, and keeping in mind God's apparent tendency to squeeze life into every possible cranny and fold, it is difficult to not believe that there's some kind of life out there, even intelligent life.

But if intelligent life lurks out there, we don't know about it, and that's odd.

Enrico Fermi, one of the great physicists of the 20th century, is known for many things: He developed the first nuclear reactor, worked on the Manhattan Project, and did important work in several branches of theoretical physics. But he is also known for the so-called "Fermi Paradox." This paradox is simply stated: If life is common in the galaxy, where is everyone? His argument is that if the galaxy hosts an abundance of life, we would know it. If even one civilization had a million-year head start on us—the briefest of times, cosmically speaking—then it should have colonized the Milky Way by now, and its presence would be obvious. But we have zero evidence of life, much less intelligent life, beyond our own fair planet.

*To keep up with recent discoveries, visit exoplanets.nasa.gov.

So, we have good reasons for thinking ET is out there, and good reasons for thinking it's not. Which is it? Both possibilities are interesting, but only the former seems to challenge traditional Christian beliefs. The Bible was written, and Christianity was developed, under the assumption that human beings were the only intelligent corporeal beings in the cosmos. If this is not true, then all kinds of questions follow.

For example, Genesis 3 says that somehow, some way, humanity has been wounded. Some commentators call Adam and Eve's disobedience a crisis of pride, some call it a fall, and some call it a coming of age. Whatever it was, our eyes were opened. We saw our own nakedness and felt shame for the first time. We were wounded, changed forever. This change is manifested (at least partly) in alienation from one another, from God, and from creation. The incarnation of God in Jesus is a divine response to that problem, a way of reconciling us to one another, to God, and to creation, of drawing us back into communion. Jesus is God's way of healing our wounds.

So, if extraterrestrial intelligence is out there, we may fairly ask: Has ET been wounded? Is ET in need of God to become incarnate on its behalf? Is there a space alien equivalent of Jesus out there somewhere? And if ET has not been wounded, how have they avoided it?

I do not know the answers to these questions, of course. They are asked merely to suggest the theological implications of extraterrestrial life. And we as Christians should take them seriously. Our God, after all, does not seem modest when it comes to the making of living things down here on Earth. And who are we to put limits on divine creativity?

Question 9
Did Galileo start the war between science and religion?

Some years ago, I led a group of students across Europe on a history of astronomy tour. We visited Krakow, Poland, where Nicholas Copernicus first considered his sun-centered model of the universe. This theory said that the Sun resides in the middle of the cosmos while all the planets, including Earth, move around it. This radical notion was opposed to the traditional earth-centered theory held in favor by the universities and by the church.

We also spent time in Prague, Czech Republic, where Johannes Kepler and Tycho Brahe fought over control of astronomical data that laid the foundation for the complete overthrow of the old earth-centered theory. But the high point of the trip was Italy, where we visited several locations relevant to the life and work of the most famous astronomer of the time, Galileo Galilei.

In Padua we walked through the room in which Galileo taught and saw the rostrum from which he lectured. We strolled through the courtyard where Galileo visited with fellow faculty members, and saw the house from which he made his first telescopic observations of the moon's mountains, the stars of the Milky Way, the strange "ears" of Saturn (later determined to be rings), and four moons of Jupiter. These observations made him a superstar in 1610.

But it was not just his observations that brought him fame. Galileo's personality, his formidable rhetorical skills, his knack for self-promotion, and his political tone-deafness had at least as much to do with his fame as his scientific aptitude. In Galileo we find a singular mix of patient and dogged observer, crystal-clear scientific thinker, razor-sharp debater, salesman, and marketer.

His marketing genius is reflected in the fact that his first book—*The Starry Messenger*, in which he revealed his earliest observations—was published in Italian. This went against the tradition of the day, which dictated that works of science and philosophy be published in Latin, the language of the learned. Opting for Italian meant that the book was available to non-experts. Galileo knew that the simple facts of lunar mountains and moons of Jupiter—outlandish ideas at the time—could be grasped by nearly anyone, even if his detailed arguments eluded many. He was a popularizer, and the science he popularized pushed up against orthodox thinking in both the academy and the church.

Later, after he had publicized his observations of the phases of Venus, Galileo began to advocate actively in favor of a sun-centered universe. This concept did more than push up against orthodoxy; it openly challenged it. University professors, followers of Aristotle and his ancient earth-centered model, were scandalized by Galileo's pronouncements about the earth being in motion around the sun. But Galileo could not be bested or out-maneuvered. With barbed wit and flourish, he easily and soundly demolished his opponents' arguments, one after another, in a series of heavily-attended public debates. This was a sure way to entertain his audience and a quick way to make lifelong enemies.

The university and the church overlapped considerably at the time, and the church got involved several years after Galileo began fighting with his fellow professors. It began in the lower ranks of the clergy. In 1614 a preacher named Caccini, in a sermon delivered in Florence, came out against Galileo. The friar's superiors reprimanded Caccini for this, but a few months later another cleric reported Galileo to the Inquisition, which, thanks to the Protestant Reformation, was operating at maximum force. The letter suggested that Galileo's scientific opinions might be heretical.

Galileo was not put on trial or condemned at this point. Moreover, Pope Urban VIII assured the scientist that he could discuss the Copernican system as a mathematical theory. (Urban had long been one of Galileo's patrons.) So, Galileo was free to discuss and teach the sun-centered model as a working hypothesis, but, as it had not been proven, he could not claim it to be a fact.

Thus, in 1624, our hero was released to throw himself into a book on the subject. Known simply as the *Dialogue*, this treatise records a conversation between three fictional characters: Salviati, who argues in favor of the Copernican model; Simplicio, a dull traditionalist who favors the geocentric system; and Sagredo, an intelligent layman who acts as a moderator between the other two. Rome granted permission for the book to be published, so long as Urban's (and thus the church's) own view was well represented.

But Galileo could not help himself. He could not resist the temptation to score points against his enemies. The *Dialogue* was purportedly a balanced presentation of both sides, but even a casual reader could discern that Galileo's beliefs came out looking very good while the opposing view was ridiculed. Moreover, Galileo made the great error of putting Urban's exact words on the subject into the mouth of the obviously inept Simplicio.

This turned many of his highly-placed defenders in Rome against him and enraged the pope, who brought the full weight of the Inquisition down on Galileo in 1633. Ultimately, he was declared "vehemently suspect of heresy" and sentenced to prison. Soon after this his sentence was commuted to house arrest and Galileo lived out the majority of his final decade at his villa in Arcetri, near Florence, working on a book about mechanics, entertaining visitors, and tending his vineyards. He died in 1642.

The whole story, which I have greatly simplified here, eventually came to be known as the "Galileo affair." Like many true accounts, it contains no simple heroes or simple villains. But Galileo stands out as a singular genius among a cast ranging from outright fools to mere luminaries.

It was not until the 19th century that the Galileo affair was spun in such a way that the church was presented as an unthinking and monolithic force of anti-intellectualism bent on extinguishing the lights of science and general progress. Two books in particular, *A History of the Conflict Between Religion and Science* by John William Draper and *A History of the Warfare of Science with Theology in Christendom* by Andrew Dickson White, relied on a selective reading of history (and not a few outright falsehoods) to promote the idea that science and Christianity are natural enemies.

Both books are avoided by serious historians today, but were initially highly influential among specialists and laypeople alike, and on both sides of the science/religion conversation. Their influence is still seen today, particularly among the so-called New Atheists who maintain that Christianity (and, indeed, all religion) is hopelessly retrogressive and opposed to science.

The reality is much more interesting than that. At Museo Galileo in Florence, my students and I saw, among other artifacts, the only two existing telescopes known to have been made and used by Galileo. The use of these devices for scientific study was encouraged by church officials early in Galileo's career, before things became difficult for all involved.

The last place we visited on our tour was Galileo's villa in Arcetri. Today it is fully restored and used for scientific workshops by the University of Florence, but when we took our walk-through, it was in some disarray, but mostly just dark and empty. It was easy to fill the spaces in my imagination. It was the first time I felt, palpably, the closeness and humanity of history. Galileo never fought against Christianity; he remained a devoted Christian his whole life. But he fathered a new way of thinking and knowing, a way that has forever changed the world.

Question 10
Does science disprove miracles?

A boy lies on his deathbed while his family prays for a miracle. His church family also prays. This congregation knows Luke 18:1-8, the parable of the persistent widow, and believes in the power of relentless prayer. So it goes for more than three weeks, 24 hours a day: a well-organized and faithful prayer effort. The people ask for a miracle. They hope for a miracle. Some, in light of the parable, expect a miracle. But in the end the boy dies. The family and congregation are heartbroken.

Stories such as this one are easily found. They are almost certainly more numerous than stories that begin similarly but have sunny endings. We ask God for miracles and we pray for miracles, but how often do they happen? Or, let's just go all the way and ask: Do miracles ever happen?

It's a natural question to ask. Miracles occur in places other than the parable in Luke, of course. The biblical world reads like a theater of the divine. Earthquakes, locust swarms, floods, and storms at sea are attributed to God. People interpreted such events theologically because there were few other ways to comprehend them. In scripture God acts everywhere, all the time, and nearly always with human beings in mind. Miracles, which scripture clearly recognizes as special cases of divine action, are easily woven into the Bible's cosmic tapestry.

Our 21st-century perspective has been shaped by much more than the Bible. Our worldviews do not conform to scripture. This is a fact, not a judgment. We see things very differently than the authors of scripture did. The world has undergone vast changes since the Bible was written. Over the last 500 years science has radically altered our view of God's creation and our place in it.

However, a number of well-known scientists insist that science disproves miracles along with God. For them science has triumphed completely and no room remains for parting seas, virgin births, wine from water, or resurrection from the dead. Since no scientific basis can be found for such events, they must not happen. Matter in motion is all, and every event is natural and has natural causes.

Scientifically-motivated atheists believe this but many others, and some Christians, believe it in their own way or suspect it on some level. After all, miracles do seem rare; suffering is widespread and arbitrary; and science explains so many things.

This may be Isaac Newton's fault. He possessed one of the truly staggering scientific minds in history. His three laws of mechanics and theory of gravity are laid out in the *Principia*, his 1687 magnum opus. In this book he claimed that objects move because external forces make them move (this is actually technically incorrect, but will suffice for our purpose). The important word here is "external": a body moves because something outside of it makes it move. The body itself has no say in the matter. There is no freedom in Newton's cosmos. Causes lead to definite effects, which themselves cause subsequent effects, and so forth. A hockey puck moves because it has been slapped by a stick, pushed by a force from outside the puck itself. It comes to rest because of friction with the ice. This force of friction is also external to the puck. Every cause produces effects in a mathematically certain way. All motion is fixed and predetermined, and no room remains for miracles.

Now imagine this mechanical viewpoint spreading out to permeate all things and all events, including human events and interactions. There are no surprises in such a universe. If we could somehow know the precise location and speed of every particle in Newton's cosmos at the present time, then we could also know the past and predict all events into the infinite future. This is Newton's vision: an impersonal mechanistic clockwork universe, so different from the God-saturated, miracle-rich cosmos of scripture.

The influence of this Newtonian worldview can hardly be overstated. The *Principia*, directly or indirectly, touched nearly every enterprise in the modern world. It birthed the Industrial Revolution and launched the Space Age. We have all absorbed Newton's work. It permeates our language. "We are Newtonians, fervent and devout, when we speak of forces and masses, of action and reaction, when we say that a sports team or a political candidate has momentum; when we note the inertia or a tradition or a bureaucracy, and when we stretch out an arm and feel the force of gravity, pulling earthward. Pre-Newtonians did not feel such a force." So writes James Gleick in his biography, *Isaac Newton*.

As influential as Newton's vision has been, more recent ideas from physics are now helping to shape our world. In the early 20th century, the science of quantum mechanics was born. Today it has matured into a pillar of science. This branch of physics, which in its way is more precise and better tested than even Newton's physics, describes remotely tiny things such as molecules, atoms, and atomic nuclei. Quantum mechanics stands in unequivocal opposition to the mechanical, cause-and-effect view of Newton. The great Englishman is no guide to the microscopic world.

Surprises abound at the quantum scale. At this level, well-defined and absolute limits circumscribe what we can know; the future is unpredictable and the past unknowable, even with perfect knowledge of the present; Newtonian cause-and-effect does not exist; matter is wavy and indefinite; particles spontaneously pop into and out of existence; and information travels instantaneously from one place to another, seemingly breaking even Einstein's cosmic speed limit.

Whatever else it does, quantum mechanics allows us a way out of Newton's cause-and-effect straightjacket. And it may be more amenable to what we call miracles. I do not mean that quantum mechanics proves that miracles happen. That would be an egregious overinterpretation. But it does allow us to reject the idea that the world is a fixed and determined mechanism.

The building blocks of matter behave strangely, but we are still relying on our Newtonian reflexes when it comes to miracles. The world is not a mechanism; it is more open and fascinating than that. The problem is not that matter is all there is, but that we think we know what matter is, and we probably don't, even after four centuries of physics. We are ignorant of so much.

Perhaps people were more gullible in years past. Perhaps they were quick to explain everything in terms of miracles. Surely science has allowed us to stop interpreting every volcano and lightning strike in theological terms. We have learned a lot, and this is not to be minimized. But perhaps our gullibility simply runs in the opposite direction than that of our ancestors. If past generations were too quick to attribute events to the direct action of God, perhaps we are too quick to attribute them to blind impersonal forces.

As great an influence as Newtonian physics has been, it, like all science, can only tell us what usually happens. And what usually happens is not the same as what always happens. We may wonder about the reality of miracles, and science may have something to do with our skepticism, but science always has limits. It is powerless to disprove any given miracle. Ultimately the question of miracles is a theological one, not a scientific one.

Question 11
How can we understand Jesus in light of evolution?

I have spoken to many church groups about faith and science. Perspectives from Old Testament books such as Genesis, Job, and Ecclesiastes often play into these discussions, but the New Testament says comparatively little about creation, so I often leave it out. Therefore, it's not surprising that, during the Q&A session, I am regularly asked some version of the question above.

Most often, the question expresses a concern that science in general, and evolution in particular, poses a threat to the centrality of Jesus Christ. When you consider billions of years of deep time, the births and deaths of stars, the great stream of evolution, the comings and goings of countless species, and the tininess and transience of human existence, where indeed does the carpenter from Nazareth fit in?

Before we start, I'd like to insist on a few fixed points about Jesus, with or without evolution. Virtually all Christian creeds affirm that Jesus (1) was born of a virgin and was simultaneously fully human and fully divine, (2) lived and taught in full accordance with the will of God, (3) suffered and died under Pontius Pilate, and (4) was resurrected from the dead on the third day. The large majority of noncreedal believers affirm these points also. For the purposes of this article, we will accept these traditional Christian claims.

We are free to do this because science (including evolution) does not disprove the Virgin Birth or the Resurrection or any other particular miracle. As I wrote in the previous chapter, science tells us—often in great detail—what usually happens, not what always happens, and the idea of a miracle is more of a theological question than a scientific one. Evolution poses no logical threat to the story outlined above. (Also, you do not need modern science to tell you that babies are not normally born without a biological father, or that dead bodies normally stay dead. Jesus' birth and resurrection surely seemed as unlikely and as surprising in 1st-century Palestine as they do in 21st-century America.)

But what does this Jesus story mean? There are no limits to the ways it might be interpreted, but traditionally we Christians have said that something about Jesus' birth, life, death, and resurrection reconciles us to God. Reconciliation is necessary because something happened in the garden of Eden, something that alienated us from God. Adam's and Eve's choices opened a great chasm between humanity and God, a chasm God has been trying to bridge ever since, and Jesus is the ultimate bridge. In particular, God reaches out to us in the Incarnation (point 1 in the story), and embraces us in the Resurrection (point 4). In this way God restores the possibility of full communion with us.

But this brief synopsis of the faith, familiar to so many, leaves out something important: creation. And Genesis 3 suggests that creation too needs reconciling. In that chapter humanity is estranged from God, but so is the natural world. "Cursed are you among all animals and among all wild creatures," God says to the serpent (v. 14). "Dust you shall eat all the days of your life." Reproduction, the central creative act of creatures, becomes painful (v. 16). The ground itself is also cursed. "In toil you shall eat of it; thorns and thistles it shall bring forth," God says to Adam (vv. 17-18). Therefore, creation is not only set against humanity, but is also alienated from God. After Gen. 3:8, the Lord, so intimate with creation before the fall, no longer walks the earth "at the time of the evening breeze."

In other words, whatever happened in the garden separated human beings and God, and separated creation from God and from us. If you visualize God, humanity, and creation as the points of a triangle, the Fall breaks the connections between all three points, and not just between us and God.

Jesus, being fully divine and fully human, naturally spans the gap between God and human beings. But does he span the gap between God and all creation? That is more difficult to see. In Jesus, God certainly entered into creation and experienced life within the material order, but only as a human being. So, the third point on the triangle—all nonhuman creatures and virtually all of created reality—is seemingly left out of God's plan of redemption.

This is where evolution comes in. Darwin's theory says that Jesus is not only related to all human beings (through Mary) but *to all of creation* (also through Mary). This is because evolution proposes that all life (including Mary) is connected to all other life.

This is one of the foundational ideas of evolution and of biology itself: If you trace our ancestry back far enough, you will see that we are related—in a literal, material way—to all life, whatever form that life takes or has taken. Therefore, since Jesus is born into the flow of evolution—that is, since he is human—then he is intimately bound up both with his human forebears and with every creature that has ever lived, no matter how alien or insignificant.

There is more. Jesus, like us, is also related to creation as a whole, and everything in it, with no exceptions. This is because biological evolution comprises only one part of an overarching, cosmic evolution that started billions of years before life began on earth. Jesus, in other words, is related to all life *and* all things. In Jesus the divine is expressed in atoms that were formed inside stars billions of ago, in molecules that predate life itself, in the DNA common to thousands of nonhuman and human generations.

When we accept the basic tenants of evolution, we see in a new way that the Incarnation reveals not only that God became human, but also that God became woven into the very fabric of all material existence. It reveals God's intimacy and love for all creation, not just the human or even the conscious part of it. And the Resurrection reveals not only God's reconciliation with all human beings, but with all life, all creatures, and all things.

Finally, the theological idea of life arising from death, so clearly a part of our faith, is echoed in the world of evolutionary science. Evolution is a brutal and bloody process, driven by death, red in tooth and claw. Every existing species and every existing creature is a result of innumerable deaths over billions of years.

Yet death is the seat of nature's creativity. Without death there is no new life. Without death no new thing happens. The beauty of evolution's creativity was not lost on its discoverer. "There is grandeur in this view of life, with its several powers, having been originally breathed into a few forms or into one; and from so simple a beginning endless forms most beautiful and most wonderful have been, and are being, evolved," wrote Darwin.

The life of the new springs continually from the death of the old, yet the new carries the mark of the old within it. This is true in evolution just as it is in theology: Jesus' resurrected body, clearly made new, was not free of scars. Yet he walked again, spoke again, laughed again, ate again, and loved again. He lived again and lives still, tipping the cosmic scales away from death and toward life. What we learn from Jesus is that death, which is so terribly present both in creation and in our personal lives, is finally no match for life.

Question 12
Do the two creation accounts in Genesis contradict each other?

Science provides a stiff challenge to those who would read Genesis 1–3 in a literal, historical way. Such a reading is plainly incompatible with a 13.8-billion-year-old, evolving cosmos. But the text itself provides its own difficulties for a historical interpretation, starting with the fact that the first three chapters of the Bible contain two separate and contradictory creation stories.

The first begins, of course, at the beginning: "In the beginning when God created the heavens and the earth…" This is the six-day creation story in which God performs different acts of creation on different days: light and dark on the first day, sky on the second, and so on. It runs through God's hallowing of the seventh day, the day of rest, in 2:3.

The second creation story begins with the next verse: "These are the generations of the heavens and the earth when they were created. In the day that the Lord God made the earth and the heavens…" This account features the creation of Eve from the rib of Adam, the trees of life and of the knowledge of good and evil, the serpent, and the disobedience of the First Couple. It continues through their expulsion from Eden at the end of chapter 3.

Contradictions appear when the stories are compared. This becomes clear when one looks at the order in which things were made. For example, the first story tells us that the animals were made before human beings. The fifth day is devoted to the creation of "swarms of living creatures" and birds that "fly above the earth across the dome of the sky." On the next day, God "made the wild animals of the earth of every kind, and the cattle of every kind, and everything that creeps upon the ground of every kind" *before* making humankind, both male and female, in the divine image.

In contrast, the second account states that Adam was the first creature to be made. Genesis 2:7 describes his creation from the dust of the earth. God breathes life into Adam, but the image of God is nowhere mentioned. It is not until Adam is in the garden, and in need of a companion, that God creates the animals and brings them to Adam. After the man finds these creatures to be insufficient as mates, God responds by forming Eve out of his rib. So, in the second account the order of creation is Adam > animals > Eve, whereas in the first it is animals > Adam/Eve (who are created simultaneously).

Other logical contradictions exist. In the first story, plants arrive before Adam. But verses 4b-7 explicitly state that God formed Adam at a time when "when no plant of the field was yet in the earth and no herb of the field had yet sprung up."

Additionally, stark stylistic differences arise between the two stories. While these do not present obvious logical problems of the kind described above, they do produce a profound contrast of atmospheres. The first account moves forward in a calm, stately, linear, liturgical, and highly ordered way. Its scope is cosmic and heaven-centered, and it describes creation in a top-down manner. The Creator is unnamed, transcendent, impersonal, distant, and abstract, creating in the divine image and by the sheer power of the spoken word. In this account there is no messiness, no trial-and-error, no sense that anything is other than good or even very good.

In contrast, the second story of creation progresses in a hit-and-miss, trial-and-error way. It has a nonlinear, messy, bottom-up quality. It is earthy and earth-centered. Here the Creator is given a name—Yahweh—and forms Adam from the dust of the ground. Yahweh then breathes life into Adam, but the divine image is not mentioned. The Creator is imminent and personal and anthropomorphic to the point of walking and talking. Additionally, and surprisingly, there is an instance in which Yahweh claims that things are "not good"—when, after Adam is placed in the garden, he is left without a companion.

Given these logical contradictions and clear stylistic and thematic differences, virtually all biblical scholars agree that these stories originate not from a single author but from different literary traditions. The first story is drawn from a later tradition than the second, and the two were eventually brought together. These sources and others are believed to be responsible for multiple tellings of other stories in the Old Testament, such as Noah's flood and Moses' ascent of Mount Sinai.

There are those who disagree that these two creation stories are separate accounts. These folks say that the two are really one, penned by a single author. A popular version of this view says that the second story is merely an up-close, zoomed-in look at the sixth day of creation. It shows the earthbound drama only, overlooked by the large-scale, cosmic, impersonal tale told in the first chapter. Those who hold this view often point to Moses as the author of Genesis 1–3, and of the rest of the first five books of the Bible (the Pentateuch).

Of course, such a view demands that one reconciles the contradictions, and this is attempted by individuals and groups alike. For example, Answers in Genesis, an organization that promotes a literal-historical view of Genesis, claims that the animals actually were formed before humankind in accordance with the first story, and that God merely brought them to Adam to be named by him in the second. But the text says otherwise. It reads, "The Lord God said, 'It is not good that the man should be alone; I will make him a helper as his partner.' So out of the ground the Lord God formed every animal of the field and every bird of the air, and brought them to the man to see what he would call them" (2:18-19a). Clearly, God's creation of the animals is a direct response to Adam's need for companionship.

Answers in Genesis resolves the plant-Adam contradiction by suggesting that the plants referred to in the second story are found only in Eden. This group claims that the phrase "plants and herbs of the field" refers to the original, barren fields of Eden, and does not refer to the world as a whole or to plants in general. In this view, green things are already growing elsewhere but not yet in the garden. Again, there is no evidence for this in the text. Therefore, such arguments have a forced, artificial quality about them.

Answers in Genesis and other groups that insist on a literal-historical interpretation of scripture force the Bible to contain no logical contradictions. But logical consistency seems to have not been a primary consideration for those who put the Bible together, whoever they were. They were certainly smart enough to have recognized these kinds of problems, but they were not terribly worried about them.

The simplest explanation for these contradictions is that there was more than one source of the Genesis text. Those who put this book in its final form apparently felt that these logical contradictions were necessary to achieve a fuller and more nuanced view of creation, of God's nature and of our relationship with God and the natural world. We see therefore that there are reasons other than science to keep us from reading Genesis in a literal-historical way. Science merely reinforces this conclusion.

Question 13
Aren't science and religion just two different things?
Why not just let each one do their own thing and leave one another alone?

The war between science and religion gets a lot of press, but many people—believers and nonbelievers alike—think the two do not overlap at all. In this view science and faith are like strangers who live in different neighborhoods, invest in different communities, and work different jobs. There is nothing wrong with being strangers, these people might say, so why try to manufacture a relationship where there is none?

One version of this perspective says that science tells us what the universe is like, and faith tells us how we should live. In his book, *Rocks of Ages: Science and Religion in the Fullness of Life*, the late biologist Stephen Jay Gould wrote, "Science covers the empirical universe: what it is made of and why does it work this way. Religion extends over questions of moral meaning and value. These two do not overlap... Science gets the age of rocks, and religion retains the rock of ages; science studies how the heavens go, and religion determines how to go to heaven" (p. 6). There is a lot to recommend of this view: It seems reasonable, it lets science be science and faith be faith, and it appeals to everyone's peacekeeping instinct. So, why fight?

Creation and evolution, for example, refer to different aspects of reality. The word "creation" implies a creator and a relationship between the creator and creation. It is an essentially theological term. Evolution, on the other hand, suggests that certain observations have been made and certain conclusions have been drawn. It is an essentially scientific term. Therefore, to ask the question, "creation or evolution?" is to make a category error.

Imagine me holding up a grapefruit and asking, "Is this grapefruit spherical, or is it yellow?" The question is obviously nonsensical because shape and color are independent qualities. You may find a spherical non-yellow fruit such as an orange, and a nonspherical yellow fruit such as a banana. Perhaps it is equally nonsensical to look at the universe and ask, "Is the cosmos created, or did it evolve?" Both can be fully true.

Moreover, you can live a long life of faithful devotion to Christ, be a pillar of your faith community, identify with and serve the poor and marginalized, work for peace and reconciliation, be a prophet of justice, and commit yourself to personal meditation and study, without knowing any science at all.

But we live in one world, not two, and finding points where science and faith overlap is not difficult. What has God made? The heavens and the earth, yes, and people too, but also *T. rex*, black holes, curved spacetime, subnuclear particles, quasar 3EG J2006–2321, neutron stars, self-organizing magnets, *E. coli*, trilobites, *archaeopteryx*, and the planet Neptune. The list goes on and on. These are the things that God has made, and it seems wrong, when thinking about creation, to not remember most of created reality. It seems wrong to insist, since these creatures and things don't matter to most people, that they must not matter to God.

But we can also ask: Who is this Christ to whom we are devoted? He is a wanderer, a teacher, and a prophet, but he is also the "firstborn of all creation, in whom all things in heaven and on earth were created, things visible and invisible" (Col. 1:15). This humble carpenter, who commanded us to serve the orphan and the widow and to pray for those who persecute us, is also the Word, the *Logos*, the organizing principle of creation itself.

We cannot claim to follow Jesus of Nazareth and turn our backs on creation.

The Bible is not content to tell the story of Jesus and throw in some color commentary. Nor does it start with the Exodus or the call of Abraham; it starts with the creation of the universe. Nor does it end with the ascension or the founding of the church, but with the end of time. Our faith sets the largest possible stage. It is about all things, and this includes science.

God calls creation "good" and "very good." It is worthy of our attention and study. Science therefore has a clear place in the Christian worldview, and, as a historical point, it is probably no accident that it arose (largely) within that view.

And when we do science, what do we learn? We learn that creation is ongoing, that it never stopped and shows no sign of stopping. We learn that we are not strangers here—we belong, we are related to all things, we are at home. But we also see, in bright detail, the danger woven into creation, from the specifics of different contagions to human-created problems such as global warming to the threats of natural disasters such as tsunamis and asteroid impacts.

This has consequences for how we think about God. Apparently, God is the kind of God whose creativity never rests, and science illuminates that process for us. God is the kind of God who creates slowly, over billions of years, gradually, indirectly. God is the kind of God who is not finished with us yet—creation never sleeps. God is the kind of God who, for whatever reason, has placed us in a good but unsafe cosmos. God is the kind of God who was incarnated into the flow of an evolving creation. God is the kind of God who generates complexity out of simplicity, and who has given creative agency to matter itself—a creative creation!

For a scientist like me, scientific knowledge helps me grow closer to God. One of my favorite ways to meditate is to take walks at night. When I do this, I receive not just the obvious beauty of the stars and planets and Milky Way; I can also visualize the nuclear reactions sustaining the stars, the iron oxide deserts and polar ice fields of Mars, the helium rain falling under Saturn's clouds, the grand rotation of our galactic pinwheel, and, on fall evenings, the Andromeda galaxy falling toward us at 70 miles per second! All of this and more fills my mind and draws me into a posture of awe, gratitude, and humility before God.

But you don't have to be a scientist to have experiences such as this; you only have to be interested. Science has taught us so much about so many things. Those hummingbirds in your backyard, those sassafras trees at the park, the moon, the rivers, the oceans—they are all treasure troves of scientific knowledge and wonder. A few minutes researching any of them will pay off for years to come with a deepened appreciation for creation and, therefore, for the Creator.

Finally, there is great practical value in recognizing and nurturing the relationship between faith and science. It is false and unhelpful to separate them. Science, taken out of its natural context of faith, grows cold and meaningless and brutal. Faith, separated from science, becomes otherworldly and sentimental and dangerous. While they may appear to be strangers, in reality they are deeply related and need one another. We separate them at our peril.

Question 14
Why do some people believe the earth is flat?

On March 24, 2019, "Mad" Mike Hughes, a California limousine driver, launched himself high above the Mojave Desert in his homemade steam-powered rocket. He reached a height of 1,875 feet and returned to the ground safely. The feat took him one step closer to his ultimate goal of rising so far up that he could see—or not see—the curvature of the earth with his own eyes.

Unfortunately for Hughes, commercial aircraft, which fly at more than 20 times his maximum altitude, do not rise high enough for passengers to detect the earth's curve with their unaided vision. Only military pilots and astronauts reach the required altitudes of 50,000-plus feet.

Hughes is not alone in his belief. The number of flat earthers has increased over the last several years. Some celebrities (for example, rapper B.o.B) are certified; others (such as basketball star Kyrie Irving) have come out as "flat curious." Flat earth groups have begun meeting in coffee houses and private residences in Denver, Boston, New York, Houston, Philadelphia, Phoenix, and Chicago. The First Annual Flat Earth International Conference was held in 2017 in Cary, N.C., followed by meetings in Edmonton, Denver, and Dallas.[1]

I find it difficult to adequately express my dismay at this trend. Unlike many ideas in science, proving the planet is spherical is not difficult. You don't need to launch yourself into space to do it. Just take a pair of binoculars to any large body of water and watch a ship sail away from shore. Through the binoculars you will see the ship disappear hull-first. The highest part of the ship will be the last part seen. And this will happen no matter which direction the ship sails. In no case will the boat simply get smaller and smaller and disappear into a point, as it would on a flat ocean.

This has been known for thousands of years. Aristotle, in the 4th century BC, provided the first formal scientific argument in favor of a spherical earth, based on three independent observations: one from the sailing ship and two from astronomy. He noted that every time the earth's shadow falls on the moon during a solar eclipse, it appears as a circle. Moreover, this was true no matter where the moon appeared in the sky. Since a sphere is the only shape that always casts a circular shadow, Aristotle had another piece of evidence in favor of a round earth.

The philosopher also knew that as he ventured south, southern stars rose while northern stars sank lower. On northward journeys the stars in the north rose and those in the south set. These facts remained no matter his longitude. This third line of evidence sealed the question for Aristotle: The earth is a ball. This was, as I have said, well over 2,000 years ago.

But today, in the most scientifically and technologically advanced nation on the planet, only 66% of adults aged 18-24 firmly believe the earth is round. For adults aged 25–34, the percentage rises to a still-shocking 76%. And it increases steadily with age: fully 94% of the 55+ cohort has never seriously questioned Aristotle's conclusion.[2] That the youngest generation would doubt such a fundamental and thoroughly verified piece of knowledge is strange, especially when that same demographic is more likely than others to accept less obvious theories such as the big bang, evolution, and global warming.

The notion that the planet is as flat as a table is surely the most glaring example of antiscientific beliefs, but others also circulate. Young earth creationism, the belief that the universe and everything in it was created in six 24-hour periods about 6,000 years ago, dismisses an enormous amount of science. Those who refuse to vaccinate their children also reject science, albeit a far smaller amount of it. The probability that human-produced greenhouse gases have driven global warming is better than 95%, but many people do not take this conclusion, or the science behind it, seriously.[3]

As a scientist, I am frustrated by these anti-science movements. But in each of these three cases I can imagine why their advocates might believe as they do. Their possible motivations do not elude me: The claims of creationists may serve to protect their idea of God. Many in the anti-vaccination movement believe vaccines cause autism and are seeking explanations and restitution for children's health problems. Climate deniers often have economic interests at stake. All of these folks have very human and easy-to-understand motivations for their rejection of science.

But what could motivate anyone to deny the shape of Planet Earth? Let's look first at those aged 18–24. As a college professor, I know two things about this group: (1) Thanks to social media, they have constant exposure to celebrities' opinions. (2) They love irony. So perhaps the recent uptick in famous flat earthers and the pleasures of satire have drawn the younger crowd. Maybe they do not really mean it.

For flat earthers as a whole, another factor comes into play. The survey cited above reveals that "most flat earthers (52%) consider themselves very religious, compared to just 20% of the general population." Perhaps the general suspicion toward science found in many traditional religious groups, the same skepticism that drives creationism, drives flat earthism as well.

Also, Genesis 1 helps. The first chapter of the Bible describes the creation of a flat earth and suggests the structure of the biblical cosmos. After the breath of God and light show up, verses 6-8 mention a dome, or firmament, that separates the "waters from the waters." God called this dome "sky." Next, flat dry land emerges from the waters below the dome. Then plants, animals, and people are added to the earth. The ancient Israelites simply described it the way they and their readers saw it. They were not trying to do science in the modern sense, but this fact seems to have passed by some flat earthers. "Why do you believe what you believe?" asks Rob Skiba, a well-known flat advocate. "There's no way you can get a spinning heliocentric globe out of anything in the Bible."[4] He's right, but he is mistaken to look to the Bible for answers he can literally discern with his own eyes.

The large number of flat earthers in the 18–24 age group cannot be explained by religious devotion, however, for this is the least religious group studied in the YouGov survey.

I suppose we should simply chalk up the rise of this weird conspiracy theory—for that is precisely what we have here—to America's overall drift away from traditional authorities, institutions, and sources of knowledge. People seem to be grasping for whatever works at the moment, and if they can get an online following and a conference out of it, all the better.

Notes

[1] www.denverpost.com/2017/07/07/colorado-earth-flat-gravity-hoax/.

[2] today.yougov.com/topics/philosophy/articles-reports/2018/04/02-most-flat-earthers-consider-themselves-religious.

[3] climate.nasa.gov/causes/.

[4] www.youtube.com/watch?v=1gHbwT_R9t0.

Question 15
As a Christian and a scientist, what do you think about atheism?

Halloween is my favorite holiday. That may sound strange coming from a Christian, but the emotional, religious, and social pressures that come during the seasons of Advent and Lent-Easter tend to shut me down. In October there's no hype and I feel free to celebrate the annual cooling of Atlanta by laughing at what scares me.

What scares me? Plenty of things. Cancer scares me. The vulnerability of my children scares me. My own weaknesses scare me. And for a number of years the so-called New Atheists scared me. I am not making this up. This group, led by the "Four Horsemen"—Richard Dawkins, Sam Harris, Daniel Dennett, and the late Christopher Hitchens—frightened me with their sustained frontal assault on all religion everywhere. Religious faith, they claim, is a mass delusion, a kind of mental disease that must be eradicated through education. They look to science to provide a worldview that, if universally accepted, will result in widespread human flourishing.

My fascination with this brand of atheism began years ago, with the publication of Harris' *The End of Faith*. I was instantly and morbidly hooked. For years I read atheist books, lurked furtively about atheist blogs, and came to know a number of atheists personally. My fascination persisted long enough to baffle me: Why should I care so much?

As a professor of physics and former working scientist, I have told myself that I care because the New Atheists claim that science—of all things—disproves God's existence. During my years as a seminary student, I told myself that I care out of theological interest. But what really scared me was the possibility that my fascination was a flag signaling my own unconscious unbelief. I gradually began to ask myself: Am I a closet atheist?

No. In my time of trying on Yes, I never felt the familiar click and closure of discovery, of having come across something true. Yet I remained unsatisfied. I could not get to the bottom of my disagreement with these people.

Then, one day a few years ago, I was leafing through my well-worn copy of William James' book, *The Varieties of Religious Experience*, when I came across—for the hundredth time—a section in which James distinguishes between two psychological types: the "healthy minded" and the "sick soul." And this time I saw clearly what separates me from the new atheists: pessimism. I saw that, if I were more optimistic, I'd probably be an atheist.

Consider the glass: Is it half-full or half-empty?

James' healthy-minded optimist regards the glass half-full by minimizing its emptiness. For this person, "the good of this world's life is regarded as the essential thing for a rational being to attend to. [The optimist] settles his scores with the more evil aspects of the universe by systematically declining to lay them to heart or to make much of them, [or] by ignoring them in his reflective calculations. Evil is a disease; and worry over disease is itself an additional form of disease, which only adds to the original complaint."[1]

In contrast, James' sick soul sees the emptiness of the glass first and can't stop wondering why it's that way. This impulse is due to the pessimist's conviction that "evil is... something radical and general... which no alteration of the environment, or any superficial arrangement of the inner self, can cure, and which requires a supernatural remedy."[2]

What truly separates me from atheism is not my belief in God, which sits a long way from the point of departure. It is instead my conviction that evil and weakness are not only problems to be solved, but also stand as reliable clues to the secret of the world. For me the emptiness of the glass is, in James' words, "the best key to life's significance, and possibly the only opener of our eyes to the deepest levels of truth."[3]

Contemporary atheism swells with optimism. Given its wall-to-wall phalanx of writers bent on mocking everything that smells of religion, it may seem that this label is ill-applied. Yet, under its bluster and iconoclasm, atheism is full of good cheer and high spirits. Anyone who knows an actual atheist knows this.

This sanguinity is likely drawn from science, which is without question the most optimistic enterprise ever concocted by human beings. Science provides contemporary atheism with a powerful alternative to religion. James writes, "The idea of [biological and cosmic evolution] lends itself to a doctrine of general meliorism and progress which fits the needs of the healthy-minded so well that it seems almost as if it might have been created for their use. Accordingly, we find [science] interpreted optimistically and embraced as a substitute for the religion they were born in."[4]

Yet, as a philosophy, science fails to satisfy. It wears blinders and refuses to acknowledge whole classes of questions that are important to regular people everywhere, questions of good and evil, and of human weakness, and of meaning. And it seems that New Atheism, in its wholesale dependence upon science as a philosophy, imports science's blinders—bound as they are to its optimism—into its worldview. And this is where the problem lies.

Imagine a clear fall Saturday in London's Hyde Park. Footballers are out; lovers doze on picnic blankets; tourists stand in clumps; university students pass by laughing. And then, over at the park's edge, behold! There passes the Atheist Bus, one of those U.K. buses that, a few years ago and with Dawkins' support, were plastered with the brightly-lettered, chirpy slogan, "There's probably no God. Now stop worrying and enjoy your life."[5]

This is the zenith of optimism. It is optimistic because it assumes that the default condition of human life is peace. It is optimistic because, in its refusal to acknowledge the deeper problems of life, it redraws human experience on a solvable and finite scale, presuming that what people really need is to "enjoy their lives." (After all, it's a beautiful day in the city. What else could there be to need?) It is optimistic because the creators of the campaign failed to imagine a poverty-stricken teenager, or a man desperate for a job, or a drug addict, or a mother who just lost a child to social services, reading their sign. They failed to consider the truly lost and lonely of the world, those who may have nothing but the faintest hope of a loving God keeping them alive.

Or maybe they did think about such a person and decided that they too need to just "stop worrying and enjoy their life"—starting with a breath of fresh, clean, godless air. Now that's optimism.

I don't buy it. And as a Christian, I'm not supposed to buy it, for it is only through the channel of pessimism—the full and unqualified acknowledgment of life's dark underside as a clear and present reality—that faith is able to do its transformative work.

The Christianity I know takes note of the blue London sky, of the footballers, and of the picnicking lovers, but it starts with the addict on the street—you know, the one optimism forgot about; the fragile one standing alone over at the edge of the park, watching the Atheist Bus roll jauntily past.

Notes

[1] William James, *The Varieties of Religious Experience* (Dover, 2002), 127.
[2] Ibid., 80.
[3] Ibid., 94.
[4] Ibid., 57.
[5] See en.wikipedia.org/wiki/Atheist_Bus_Campaign.

Question 16
What do you think about global warming?

With the exception of our own dear Earth, the planet Mars has, over the last half century, become the most visited, the most probed, the most orbited, the most closely inspected, the most roved-over, and the most photographed object in the solar system. We have made countless discoveries about its topography, its weather, its seasonal dynamics, its harboring of water and organic compounds, and its geology past and present. Mars will be the first planet inhabited in any future colonization of the solar system, and it stands as a symbol of the possibility of extraterrestrial life.

Mars has so overshadowed the game of planetary exploration that it's easy to forget it was not the first planet to be flown by or visited. Nor was it the first to be orbited or landed upon or to have its atmosphere analyzed, its winds clocked, or its landscape photographed. The Soviet *Venera* program, which lasted from 1961 to 1984, achieved all of this with Venus well before the United States' *Viking 1* touched down on Mars in July 1976.

You may wonder why, despite not being the first investigated, Mars has come to the forefront of our planetary exploration while Venus has languished in obscurity. It's not because of Venus' distance, or its size, or its gravity. It's not because Venus rotates so slowly (once every 225 Earth days) or because it contains traces of sulfur dioxide in its atmosphere. It's because, while Mars chills at an average of -80°F, Venus broils at 870°F. At this temperature lead melts, electronics cannot function more than a few hours, and life cannot exist. And make no mistake: the exploration of the solar system is all about life—ours included.

Venus' proximity to the sun and its thick atmosphere help drive up the planet's temperature. But these alone are insufficient to make it so hot; only when you consider the composition of the atmosphere—96.5% carbon dioxide—does it begin to make sense, because this gas (abbreviated CO_2) absorbs heat very efficiently.

Carbon dioxide makes up only about 0.04% of the earth's atmosphere but, from the point of view of climate, it plays an outsized role. If it were not present, the earth would be about as cold as Mars. But this is not our concern because, due to deforestation and the burning of fossil fuels, the amount of CO_2 in our atmosphere is increasing. Even a small boost translates into large-scale global changes: Since the late 19th century, the surface temperature of the earth has risen by about 1.6°F, and this trend is accelerating. Most of the warming has occurred over the last 35 years, with the seven hottest years on record occurring since 2010. We'll never become Venus, but we're moving steadily in that direction.

This increase—1.6°—may not seem like much, but when it's spread out over the planet it adds up to an enormous amount of energy. In response, the oceans have risen about 8 inches over the last century, largely due to thermal expansion. Much of the CO_2 has been absorbed by those same oceans; since the beginning of the Industrial Revolution the acidity of the seas has risen by about 30%. The consequences for marine life are dire. Other consequences of global warming include more extreme highs and lows and increased frequency and intensity of severe weather events. A marked decrease in the extent and thickness of arctic sea ice has been documented. There is less snow cover in winter. Glaciers are retreating. Vast sections of Antarctic ice shelves are calving every summer and are not being replaced during colder months. The potential consequences of the continuation of global warming to human health and happiness, to political and technological systems, and to nonhuman life, are severe.

It is 95%–100% certain that human influence has been the dominant cause of observed warming since 1950, and these findings have been recognized by the national science academies of all major industrialized nations and are not disputed by any national or international scientific body. Therefore, as a scientist and citizen of the world, I understand and accept global warming as a legitimate and looming problem.

As a Christian, how do I think about global warming? It may sound strange to say, but I start with the claim, made in Genesis 1, that we are "created in the image of God." What does this phrase mean? Many answers have been suggested over the centuries, but *dominion* has something to do with it. This is made clear in Gen. 1:26-27:

> Then God said, "Let us make humankind in our image, according to our likeness; and let them have dominion over the fish of the sea, and over the birds of the air, and over the cattle, and over all the wild animals of the earth, and over every creeping thing that creeps upon the earth." So God created humankind in his image, in the image of God he created them; male and female he created them.

Unfortunately, the word "dominion" has the same root as "dominate," so it often carries the suggestion of tyranny or plunder or subjugation. Therefore, this concept of the divine image is fraught with difficulty.

But as Christians we are often called to interpret the Old Testament through the lens of the New Testament, and in Matthew 20 we find a story to shed light on this question of dominion.

It is late in Jesus' ministry. He has set his face toward Jerusalem and explained to the disciples that he will be arrested, crucified, and killed. But the disciples aren't hearing it; they're too busy trying to figure out which among them is the greatest. James and John figure it must be one of them so, as brothers will, they fight it out.

Eventually they send their mother to ask Jesus about it for them. (Yes, they made their mother do it!)

She approaches Jesus and says, "Declare that these two sons of mine will sit, one at your right hand and one at your left, in your kingdom." Jesus answers, "You do not know what you are asking. Are you able to drink the cup that I am about to drink?" James and John reply, because they're standing right behind Mom, "We are able." Jesus said, "You will indeed drink my cup, but to sit at my right hand and at my left, this is not mine to grant, but it is for those for whom it has been prepared by my Father."

The other disciples hear this conversation and grow angry. Either they think James and John are wrong to ask the question in the first place or they believe themselves to be the greatest. In any case, Jesus calms everyone down by saying, "You know that the rulers of the Gentiles lord it over them, and their great ones are tyrants over them. It will not be so among you; but whoever wishes to be great among you must be your servant, and whoever wishes to be first among you must be your slave; just as the Son of Man came not to be served but to serve."

God is a servant, not a tyrant, and the divine image in us calls us to serve. This radical piece of theology sits at the foundation of a faithful response to global warming. Old notions of dominion as domination vanish in the light of this call. In Jesus' upside-down ethic we are to rule not by subjugation or plunder of natural resources but by service. Just as God preserves and provides for all creatures, we are to preserve and provide for all creatures. We are to humble ourselves, seek forgiveness for our sins against the created order, and work diligently in the service of one another, of God, and of the fish of the sea, and the birds of the air, and the cattle, and all the wild animals of the earth, and every creeping thing upon the earth.

Question 17
Are our beliefs about God just patterns of neurons firing in our brains and nothing more?

Keith, my brother-in-law, is a Baptist like me. Unlike me, however, he spent a number of years in the Episcopal Church. One of the things he'll tell you is that Baptists know how to teach children and Episcopalians know how to teach teenagers. Baptists tell the story to little ones in a hundred creative and memorable ways but, on the whole, Episcopalians do better when the waters get deeper and the questions grow difficult.

I can't speak for Episcopalians, but I can affirm—for my case at least—the Baptist piece. I was raised a Baptist and got a good sense of the story as a child, but things got a little vague as I entered the youth group: there was no confirmation process, and I never felt that church was a good place to ask my questions.

But today I'm beginning to think we Baptists should teach our children the value of periodically challenging their beliefs about God, in part because of the way our brains work.

Recently I ran across a video* that shows, through a perfectly transparent demonstration, the power of unchallenged ideas and the difficulty of changing the way we think.

In the video a fellow named Destin Sandin tries to ride a bicycle. At first glance the bike looks normal, but the handlebars are connected to the front tire via a simple gear system in such a way that the bike goes left when the rider turns right, and right when the rider turns left. It is a backwards bicycle.

Destin tries to ride it but fails spectacularly and repeatedly. His brain is simply not wired for the job. As a youngster he learned to ride a bike and over years of riding, that skill—that way of thinking—became entrenched, hardwired into his brain. The associated neural pathways hardened, and using them became automatic. And then a new situation was encountered in which the old skill and old pathways not only failed but also actively confounded his efforts. Destin eventually learns how to ride the backwards bike, but it requires eight months of steady practice. It is not easy to rewire one's brain.

I suspect that, like knowing how to ride a bike, ideas about God often become fixed at a young age. Kids may innately believe in God, but I'm not talking about belief versus disbelief. I'm talking about what kids—and the grownups they become—believe *about* God. In many cases, and perhaps most often when children are taught to not question their own beliefs, whatever one is taught about God at a young age persists for a lifetime.

---

*See vimeo.com/157192392.

Like all other concepts and skills, our ideas about God are associated with particular sets of neural pathways in our skulls. Large parts of these concepts and pathways are certainly products of our early experiences and educations and become hardwired as surely as Destin's bike-riding knowledge.

Maybe your idea of God's love is deeply influenced by your parents' devotion and constancy. Perhaps your belief in a watchful God is the result of a childhood in which you were granted no privacy. It may be that your concept of God's judgment is wrapped up in the story of Noah's flood, which used to give you nightmares. And maybe the nativity story has prompted you to see God in out-of-the-way people and places.

These theological ideas stay with us and, over time, the neural pathways associated with them become fixed and difficult to change. But do our beliefs last because they're true or because that's just the way our brains work?

Sorry for the ambivalence, but it's a little of both: God exists—whatever the word "exists" might mean in reference to God. Put another way, I don't use the word "God" as a high-level reference or metaphor for certain kinds of neural activity, or for the "really real" brain. One of the reasons the God concept has been so successful and has survived for so long in so many social contexts is because there is something to it. God is real.

But concepts—not reality—will, in the best of circumstances, change when they are sufficiently challenged. And changing our idea of God means, among many other things, an actual physical rewiring of the brain, which is difficult to do.

Just ask Destin, who encountered a new situation in which his old ideas simply did not work. In fact, his old ideas aggressively frustrated his success. When a particular God-concept is seriously challenged, we can remake our concept to fit the new reality. (Alternately, we can resign ourselves to falling over, or to running into walls, or to becoming fundamentalists.) It could be the death of a loved one, an addiction, the story of a pastor who molests an acolyte, or an intellectual challenge that threatens the old God-idea. It could be anything, really.

My Baptist upbringing painted God as a powerful and inscrutable yet ultimately loving white man in the sky. No one ever told me this in so many words, of course, but that's pretty much what all the church language, taken together, pointed to. God was a cosmic, omnipotent king who watched over us every day and kept tabs on us and went to great lengths to care for us and keep us all safe and happy.

I don't believe this anymore, and the shift didn't happen overnight. It took Destin months to unlearn his bike-riding knowledge, but it took me years to unlearn my original God-concept.

The final minutes of the video deliver the real punchline: After learning how to ride the backwards bike, Destin can no longer ride a normal one. In learning a new skill, not only did he create some new circuitry in his brain; simultaneously, the old circuitry eroded, presumably from disuse.

Contrary to the wisdom of the ages, it is possible to forgot how to ride a bike.

Dustin eventually relearns how to ride a normal bicycle, but it takes more time and more spills. And when he rides a normal bike today, it's not easy. He has to think about it. In the video Destin looks at the camera and says with a smile, "I can't ride a bike like you can anymore."

Once you expand your horizons—whether bike-oriented or theological—some things that used to be simple and intuitive become less so.

Question 18
What is the best academic class you ever took?

I spent my first two undergraduate years at Young Harris College, a tiny institution in the Blue Ridge Mountains of North Georgia. Those years affected me profoundly on a personal and emotional level, but also on an educational level. Young Harris offered me clean air, quiet nights, and an opportunity to exercise my mind freely, without the distractions and weird social pressures of high school. I loved it all—literature, history, calculus, even physical education. But two classes in particular opened my mind to worlds beyond my own: Religion 101 and Astronomy 101.

The first was a survey of the world's great religions. I had spent my life in a Baptist church and graduated from a Catholic high school but, aside from attending a single bar mitzvah in 5th grade, knew nothing of the world beyond Christianity. The professor took us on a global religion tour, spending a couple weeks each on Hinduism, Taoism, Confucianism, Buddhism, Judaism, Islam, and Christianity.

Aside from Christianity, Judaism was the most familiar. I felt at home with its scripture, its precepts of justice and righteousness, its creation story, its prophets, and its God. It seemed strange that Jews still awaited the Messiah, but I was not unsettled by this difference. Judaism struck me as recognizably religious and basically unsurprising.

Islam took me a few steps further from the customary: when we turned to it, my fascination began to grow. Here was a global religion founded by a singular personality, a historical figure like Jesus himself, who counted Jesus as a prophet and who claimed that his own expression of monotheism—not that of the Jews, not that of the Christians—was the true one. Adam showed up in the Quran, as did Noah, Abraham, Sarah, Isaac, Ishmael, Mary, Jesus, and many others, but their stories diverged from the familiar ones in ways that seemed important. The Five Pillars of Islam, the fundamental obligations of all practicing Muslims, seemed refreshing and straightforward when compared to the old "invite Jesus into your heart" business I had grown up with in the Baptist church, which was hard on my nerves.

But these differences were as nothing compared to those I discovered between the Eastern and Western traditions. A deep conceptual abyss lies between these worlds of religious thought. Where Judaism, Christianity, and Islam come down hard and clear with monotheism, their Eastern cousins posit hundreds of millions of gods or zero gods. To the Western mind, Eastern theology grows hazy or doesn't seem to exist at all. I was taught that Hinduism is largely unorganized, has no central personality or formal structure or absolutely canonical scriptures, makes room for whatever local gods happen to arise, and permits individuals as many lifetimes as they need to attain full spiritual awakening. Buddhism is centered on a single personality but expresses itself across a wide spectrum of belief and disbelief (even outright atheism), action and inaction, words and silences.

As a 19-year-old who had had only the vaguest experiences with his nearest-neighbor religion, all of this exhilarated and destabilized me. It exhilarated me because it was so new and mind-expanding, but it destabilized me because it gave the clear impression that, when it comes to religion, no one really knows anything. It seemed that everyone on the planet was just making it up as they went along. How could I trust the claims of any religion at all?

I would receive some answers to this question the following year when I took Astronomy 101. Actually, *answers* is not quite right: Astronomy 101 offered me *perspective*.

Sitting in the college planetarium, I learned about Jupiter's magnetic field, the Oort cloud, stellar spectroscopy, Hubble's law, and all the rest. But these bits of knowledge themselves, fascinating though they are, did not offer perspective—at least not when taken one by one. Perspective came when they were all put together into a single, unified, large-scale vision of the cosmos. The details served to make the big picture real, believable, and terribly exciting to me.

It's easy, as human beings fixed to the surface of our little planet, to forget the cosmos. We live deep in the human mix and rarely take a breath, step away, look up, and take the larger view.

Back in August 2017, a total solar eclipse passed across the face of North America and amazed people from Oregon to South Carolina. This event evoked wonder and brought an enlarged perspective for everyone who witnessed it. As I viewed the eclipse with my family (at Young Harris of all places), I recalled this quote from Horace Mann: "Astronomy is one of the sublimest fields of human investigation. The mind that grasps its facts and principles receives something of the enlargement and grandeur belonging to the science itself. It is a quickener of devotion."

The astronomical perspective, if held earnestly in the mind over months and years, produces several effects. First, by demonstrating the limits of our influence and power, it produces humility. Second, it encourages wonder and reveals the miraculous nature of all things. Third, it shows, without ambiguity, that human beings are much more alike than we are different.

Each of these lessons finds an application in our approach to the world's religions. First, we find ourselves on this tiny planet lost among an infinity of galaxies and time unimaginable. This knowledge produces an ironic effect: We realize we are subject to forces far beyond our control and, in reality, we know very little. The knowledge we do possess, much of it religious, is provisional or limited or uncertain.

Second, the cosmos teases us with its beauty and essential strangeness. If the universe is a bottomless well of mystery, so too is the God who continues to create it. Not one of us, Christian or otherwise, knows God fully.

Third, all human beings seek transcendence, that is, connection with one another and with God. We notice our differences only because we are so fundamentally alike. You wouldn't spend time commenting on the surprising differences between a sparrow, a semi-truck, and a strong cup of coffee. It would never occur to you to do so. Our underlying sameness makes our differences obvious. The same is true, I believe, of our religions. All of them, no matter how odd-seeming, are good and outward signs of the core human drive for transcendence.

Christians have a responsibility to learn about as many religions as possible, and as deeply as possible—we live in a religiously plural society and knowing our neighbors is an essential part of loving them. But we must also come to know our own faith better. After all, if you're looking for water, it's better to dig a single deep well than 10 shallow ones. Here's the good news: learning about other religions makes knowing your own not only possible, but also inevitable. You never see your own view clearly until you take a good hard look at the world through another's eyes. And when you return to your own, as you always do, you will know it as never before.

Astronomy 101 offered me a new, mind-blowing perspective from which I could get above the human fray and see humanity anew, in all our religious variation and unity—a perspective from which the provisional nature of knowledge is made clear, and a perspective in which the mystery of God is always magnified.

Question 19
What was the Star of Bethlehem?

The opening verses of Matthew 2 tell us that "in the time of King Herod, after Jesus was born in Bethlehem of Judea, wise men from the East came to Jerusalem, asking, 'Where is the child who has been born king of the Jews? For we observed his star at its rising, and have come to pay him homage.'" When Herod heard this, he grew frightened and tried to deceive the wise men. He "sent them to Bethlehem, saying, 'Go and search diligently for the child; and when you have found him, bring me word so that I may also go and pay him homage.' When they had heard the king, they set out; and there, ahead of them, went the star that they had seen at its rising, until it stopped over the place where the child was. When they saw that the star had stopped, they were overwhelmed with joy" (vv. 8-10).

This is the only passage in which the so-called Star of Bethlehem appears in the Bible. None of the other gospels mention it, and no other biblical writings refer to it. But this one passage has driven a small industry of speculators, mathematicians, astronomers, and biblical scholars to determine, as best they can, the precise nature of this celebrated celestial event. Many explanations have been put forward, and five of the top contenders are outlined below.

Star. This seems quite unlikely. Normal stars do not appear suddenly from nowhere. The wise men, who were really astrologers, were intimately familiar with the night sky and would not have been surprised or even particularly interested in the regular appearance of even the brightest of known stars. Something more unusual must have motivated them to leave their homeland and travel west.

Supernova. Certain massive stars die in dramatic blazes of radiation called "supernovas." These shine extremely brightly—a million times brighter than the original star—for a month or two and then gradually fade. Throughout recorded history several bright supernovas have been witnessed by human beings with their unaided eyes, the most recent having occurred in February 1987. Some astronomers believe the Star of Bethlehem could have been such an event, but this theory comes with two problems.

First, there is no record in any world culture of a bright supernova anywhere near the time of Jesus' birth, and second, such an explosion would have left behind a conspicuous telltale object called a "supernova remnant." Any 2,000-year-old remnant would be pretty easy for astronomers to find, unless the explosion occurred on the far side of the Milky Way, in which case the supernova itself would not have been particularly bright, if it could be seen at all. In any case, no remnant of that age has been uncovered in the part of the sky visible to observers in the Near East.

It could have occurred in a neighboring galaxy, but this remains a highly speculative theory.

Comet. Comets are icy bodies that orbit the sun. It is estimated that about a trillion of them exist in the solar system, and a remotely tiny fraction of them are visible with the unaided eye. Halley's Comet is the best-known example. Comet periods, that is, the times required for a full orbit, span a vast range of values. Halley returns every 75.3 years—it last passed through the inner solar system in 1986 and will return in 2061—but most require much more time to complete a single orbit. A bright comet could have passed through the sky at the time of Jesus' birth and it may not be back for 10,000 years or even much longer—if it returns at all. Astrologers everywhere would have noticed it and found it significant: before the scientific era, comets were considered to herald special events.

One problem with this theory is that the gospel writer described the object as a star, and most comets appear as fuzzy blobs and have long bright tails and look nothing like stars. It's possible, however, that the author or the ancient Greek language itself did draw such a distinction. Also, comets were generally seen as bad omens and portents of doom, which of course is not how the magi interpreted the star.

Planetary conjunction. Planets travel among the stars and occasionally pass one another. When two or more planets appear in the same small area of the sky, it's called conjunction. In 3 BC Venus and Jupiter—the two brightest planets—passed one another in the constellation Leo. This would have been noticeable by anyone, and the magi would have known it was coming. And, occurring as it did in Leo, this conjunction may have signaled an event connected to royalty. (The brightest star in Leo is Regulus, as in "regal.")

You may think that since this conjunction happened in 3 BC it could not be taken seriously as an explanation for the Star of Bethlehem. Was not Jesus born in the year AD 1? No. It has been known since the early 17th century, when Johannes Kepler took up the problem, that the Nativity occurred well before this date. Depending on who you ask, Jesus was born anywhere between 8 and 3 BC.

Although this particular theory has a lot in its favor, it is not without one tiny problem: Though Jesus could have been born anytime between 8 and 3 BC, calculations show that the most likely date for his birth is 4, not 3, BC. Still, it seems quite plausible.

Literary trope. A trope is any commonly-used metaphor or symbol or literary motif. Old stories of the births of great kings and emperors often featured celestial events, whether or not these events were historical. A large number of legends concerning miracles and portents were floating about the Roman Empire at the time Augustus was born, in 63 BC; perhaps this tradition was picked up by Matthew. (Mark, widely believed to be the first gospel written, makes no mention of the star or the magi.)

Adding the star to the story would make the point that Jesus' birth was important enough to alter history. It would also help place Jesus in the category of Son of God, which was a name used by many powerful rulers in Rome and the ancient Near East. Therefore, claims in the Gospels that Jesus was the Son of God carried both political and religious weight. This final explanation is the one favored by most biblical scholars.

***

So, we have several options, and we could list others too: a heliacal rising of a star, in which a bright star appears in the east just before sunrise; a double occultation that occurred in 6 BC, in which Jupiter passed behind the moon twice in a short amount of time; and even some kind of UFO.

None of these theories come without logical or scientific problems, except for the literary trope. I leave it to you to decide which you like the most. I certainly don't believe that this is a crucial point for Christians to agree on; for me it lands in the ballpark of "fun to think and talk about but not to take too seriously." If I were forced to choose a scientific explanation, however, I would favor the conjunction for its predictability and regal overtones. But when I read the Nativity narrative, I usually do not think in strict literal or historical terms, so the literary trope also appeals to me.

Question 20
Were biblical years shorter than our current years?

We all know about the birth of Adam; he was made by God "from the dust of the ground," according to Gen. 2:7. But we don't talk about his death very often, even though the Bible mentions it. In Gen. 5:5 we read that, after having Cain, Abel, Seth, and a number of other children with his wife Eve, "all the days that Adam lived were nine hundred thirty years; and he died." 930 years!

There's more. All of Adam's descendants mentioned in Genesis 5 lived enormously long lives; the shortest life was that of Enoch, who lived 365 years. Most had lives much nearer in length to that of Methuselah, who, at 969 years, is the longest-lived person in the Bible.

The genealogy in Genesis 5 takes us through Noah, who became the father of Shem, Ham, and Japheth at the nimble age of 500 years. After this he lived 450 more years, for a total of 950. Then, post-flood, the average age gradually declines until we finally get to Abraham's death in Genesis 25, where we read that he lived only 175 years.

According to the Bible, the average length of human life eventually wound down past Abraham's 175 to the more standard lifespan noted in Ps. 90:10, "The days of our life are seventy years, or perhaps eighty, if we are strong."

What does all this mean? How can it be that human beings lived so long, and why would the length of life shorten so dramatically after the flood? You'll not be surprised to know that several theories have been proposed to explain all of this.

Some scholars have suggested that these ages of 900-plus years have been created by mistakes in translation. Perhaps the word for "year" had different meanings to those Greeks who first translated Genesis; perhaps it meant a season (three lunar cycles) or a month (a single lunar cycle). This understanding of the word was acknowledged by none other than Augustine.

The problem with this view is that, though it works in some cases for the overall life spans of the early patriarchs, it does not make sense of the ages at which they begot children. For example, if we take Adam's age at death and divide it by 12, we find that he would have lived a total of 77 years. This makes sense. But using the same logic, he would have fathered Enoch at age 11. Similar problems arise if we convert using seasons instead of months. Therefore, this theory seems unlikely.

Other scholars have put forth astronomical explanations. One of these involves the rotation rate of the earth, which is not constant. The earth has in fact slowly transferred angular momentum to the moon, sending the moon further away from the earth and increasing the length of our days. One consequence of this phenomenon is that people long ago would have lived through more days than we do now.

Two problems immediately arise. First, though the length of the day has changed, the length of the year has not, and the ancients would have known the same cycle of seasons and they would have lasted a single year. Therefore, on a rapidly rotating earth they would have lived through more days but not through more years. Second, the length of the day is growing longer very gradually. Today is only about two milliseconds (that's 1/500th of a second) longer than the same calendar day 100 years ago. This means that there were about 420 days per year about 400,000,000 years ago, long before human beings made their appearance in the cosmos. The effect is far too subtle to account for such dramatically long lifespans.

Perhaps these numbers—930 for Adam, 912 for Adam's son Seth, 905 for Seth's son Enosh, and so on—are not meant to be literal but are instead symbolic in the same way that the numbers 3, 7, 12, and 40 are symbolic numbers in the Bible. This is yet another possible explanation. At face value this seems unlikely: What possible significance could there be to numbers such as the ones listed above, and to others that appear in Genesis 5 (ex.: 910, 895, 962, 365, and 969)? Some researchers have suggested that, in the Babylonian system of numbers, based as it is on the number 60 (and not 10 as ours is), these lifespans are important symbols with hidden meanings.

The trouble with this theory is that, other than a few numerical coincidences, no support can be found for it. No other part of scripture has any relation to the Babylonian system of numbers, and no extrabiblical sources back up this claim.

Yet another idea to explain these numbers is that the ages do not indicate spans of individual lives but the length of time that tribes, dynasties, or clans exercised dominion. But this theory is contradicted by some of the details of the stories of the patriarchs and also has no biblical or extrabiblical support.

Of course, many people reject all these theories and believe that if the Bible says Adam lived 930 years, then that's how long Adam lived. To them the simplest explanation is that the early patriarchs really did live long lives. Their reasoning goes something like this: Human beings were made to live forever, but when we were shut out of Eden, we no longer had access to the fruit of the Tree of Life and therefore became mortal. Early on we were nearer to our primeval state of sinlessness so we lived longer, but over time we fell further from the Edenic bliss for which we were designed and the corrupting effect of sin accumulated slowly and ate away at our longevity.

But reading the Bible like this, as word-for-word physical truth, is not possible if one takes science seriously. We know that the human race is far older than the 6,000 years demanded by such a literal reading and there is no evidence that people in the Bronze Age—the time of the patriarchs—lived much beyond 40 or 50 years. Every line of scientific inquiry leads us to believe that the average human lifespan has only increased with time.

The problem at hand is most easily resolved when you realize that, at the time Genesis was written, there was no recorded history in the modern sense of the word. Genesis 1–11, the so-called *primeval history*, tells stories that run from the creation of the cosmos to the introduction of Abraham. These tales were passed down from one generation to the next orally; literacy was extremely rare, and even those who *could* read and write did not emphasize factual, detailed record-keeping the way we do today. The writers were not intent on telling the literal, physical history of Israel but in crafting a story that would make sense of the vast gulf of time that preceded them. The long lives of the early patriarchs were likely meant to span that gulf while at the same time assisting people as they sought to understand their past and their relationship to God.

In other words, it is not really possible, or even responsible, to read Genesis 1–11 literally. These stories are meant to teach about the foundations of morality and our relationships with God, creation, and one another, and to establish Israel within a cosmic theological narrative. They are more poetic than physical or factual, but please remember: This does make them untrue, but it makes them vessels of truths that transcend simple, literal language

Question 21
Why should people of good faith encourage scientific understanding?

The early days of the Covid-19 pandemic led to the closure of schools, restaurants, stores, and businesses of all kinds. It forced concerts, performances, and festivals to be cancelled. Airports, interstates, and shopping malls were nearly empty for weeks. Virtually all private vacations and all public events were taken off the books. Globally, life ground to a halt. Scientists told us that social distancing was the key to slowing down the spread of this virus, and most people in most places believed them and acted accordingly.

But others publicly questioned the scientific consensus and disregarded the recommendations of those professionals who have committed their lives to understanding infectious diseases. Many of these people were motivated by religion.

"We are exercising our right as people of faith to worship," said Wilbur Browning, senior pastor of Centennial Olivet Baptist Church in Louisville, Ky., when asked why he refused to close his church on Easter Sunday. "According to the First Amendment, last time I read it, the governor can't intervene to tell us how to worship our God. I'm a man of God and we believe in God, so coronavirus, for us, has not taken a place of the power of God in our life."[1]

In a note to the congregation, Browning wrote: "By now all have heard of the Coronavirus and the number of people it has affected. Let us be reminded whatever God allows is purposeful... In light of this, we have prayerfully decided not to close the church. This is... not a time to shrink back, but to move forward, prayerfully and faithfully in the Lord Jesus Christ, who reminded us that tribulations and suffering would surely come."[2]

Kentucky Governor Andy Beshear, who ordered the closing of houses of worship along with restaurants and other businesses in early 2020, was not amused. During a news conference Beshear said of another Kentucky church that refused to close: "It's a scientific fact that [the pastor] holding this service today will spread the virus within his congregation, and at Christmas, he's going to have fewer people in his congregation."[3]

Politics played a significant part in this resistance movement. Many people, like Pastor Browning, who resisted government authority did so out of a sense that their constitutional freedoms were being eroded by orders to stay at home. And, since the government was following the advice of the scientific establishment, scientists were rejected alongside elected officials.

But the religious motivation cannot be denied, and the rejection of science by people of faith is nothing new: Creationism is explicitly religious. The anti-vaccination movement has a large religious representation. Many people reject climate science for religious reasons. Therefore, the trend of religiously motivated skepticism of shelter-in-place orders in the early days of Covid-19, backed as they were by science, was just a new variation on an old theme.

People died and more lives were at stake. So, why do so many Christians reject science?

Theologies that emphasize the distinction between the wisdom of humanity and the power of God may motivate such rejections by placing science in the "wisdom of humanity" category. In 1 Cor. 2:4-5 Paul writes: "My speech and my proclamation were not with plausible words of wisdom, but with a demonstration of the Spirit and of power, so that your faith might rest not on human wisdom but on the power of God." To attribute wisdom and authority to scientists is to attribute power to the virus, but as Browning said, "coronavirus, for us, has not taken a place of the power of God in our life."

But interpreting Paul this way and in this context reminds me of that old story you have almost certainly heard before: A downpour begins and a man's house starts to flood. A neighbor stops by in her car and says, "We're moving to higher ground!" The man replies, "No, God will save me!" When the water reaches nine feet, he's in his second-story window and a boy paddles up in a canoe. "Climb in!" says the boy. "No, God will save me!" replies the man. When the water reaches 18 feet, the man has crawled up on the roof and a helicopter stops overhead. "Climb up!" shouts the pilot as a ladder is lowered. "No, God will save me!" replies the man. So, the man drowns and goes to heaven and asks God, "Why didn't you save me?" to which God replies, "I tried—three times!"

Among some American Christians there seems to be a sense that God's saving work must come from inside the church or carry some miraculous or otherworldly elements. But this is just magical thinking, because God often speaks to us through the everyday and the nonreligious: a neighbor, a helicopter pilot, a scientist on TV.

Scripture should never be interpreted in ways that directly contradict our best knowledge about the world and the way it works, whether it is Genesis and evolution or 1 Corinthians and epidemiology.

Science remains our best way of learning about the biological and physical world. To pursue science is to exercise one's God-given capacity to learn and know and understand, directed toward God's very good creation. Science can even be a way of loving God. "You shall love the Lord your God with all your heart, and with all your soul, and with all your *mind*," said Jesus in Matt. 22:37. The pursuit of science, which is but one form of the intellectual love of God, is nothing less than worship for a scientist who is also a Christian. St. Augustine wrote, "A person who is a good and true Christian should realize that truth belongs to his Lord, wherever it is found,"[4] and this includes any and all truth, whether it's discovered in church, in school, at the observatory, in the physics lab, or at the CDC (Centers for Disease Control).

Christianity has not always been true to its foundational beliefs, two of which are: (1) God created the world and called it very good, and (2) Jesus of Nazareth is God incarnate. These statements of faith both point to a biological and physical world of radical goodness and value, a world that God created and entered, a world in which God became embodied in flesh and bone. We have no place to call the world anything but blessed, good, reliable, and knowable: the terrific success of science underlines this truth.

Science has been called the kingdom of facts. This oversimplifies things, but I like it nonetheless. In my view, facts are divine gifts, fixed points in an ever-turbulent world. I mean this exactly as I say it—facts are literally gifts from God, and gifts are meant to be shared and passed on. Here's one fact, for example: Until vaccines became available, social distancing and masking were the only way to beat the Covid-19 virus and save lives. To reject science is to reject these divine gifts, and in this age, to reject them may mean death.

Notes

[1] See bit.ly/2YiBLmD.

[2] Ibid.

[3] fox5sandiego.com/news/trending/kentucky-pastor-plans-to-hold-easter-service-despite-virus-orders/.

[4] Augustine of Hippo, *On Christian Doctrine*, II, 18. See, e.g., faculty.georgetown.edu/jod/augustine/ddc.html.

Question 22
Doesn't it take faith to believe in science?

The sentiment that it requires faith to believe in certain scientific theories is one I have come across many times in my work as a writer and speaker. It does seem, on the face of things, that, just as we call on faith to believe the tenets of Christianity, we also must rely on faith to believe things such as the big bang, or evolution, or relativity. But I don't think that's really true.

Let's first look at core Christian beliefs. Orthodox Christianity asks us to believe that there exists an all-loving, all-powerful divine being, God, who created the world at some time in the past and who is present with us now. Human beings carry the image of this creator within us. But we have somehow become alienated from this same God, who wants to be reconciled to us. With this goal, God has reached out to us again and again throughout history and, about two thousand years ago, actually became one of us.

God was incarnated in a working-class, Palestinian-Jewish man named Jesus, who grew up in a no-name town on a forgotten fringe of the Roman Empire. Jesus became an itinerant preacher and healer and was ultimately tortured and killed by the religious and political authorities. He didn't stay dead, however. He rose from the grave a few days after he was killed and then ascended into heaven. Eventually the Holy Spirit, who is also God, fell upon those who had followed Jesus, and is with us still. The upshot of this whole affair is that we are now reconciled to God.

This seems a little hard to believe, but as Christians we accept it on faith. When we turn to science, we find a collection of theories that seem as implausible as the picture described above. Consider the following, for example:

- The *big bang* asks us to believe that about 13.8 billion years ago everything that existed somehow exploded out of an infinitesimally small, infinitely hot, infinitely dense point and has been expanding and cooling ever since.
- *Evolution* states that all life is related, and not in a vague way but according to the exact meaning of the word: Long-extinct lizards, fish, worms, and single-celled organisms are your ancestors. Present-day house cats and narwhals and rotifers and *e. coli* and hickory trees are your relatives.
- Einstein's theory of *relativity* proposes that both time and space are flexible and not absolute; that time slows down when you travel at high speeds and as you draw near massive objects; that distances between things vary as your speed changes; and that these effects are not optical illusions or products of poor measurements, but are real physical facts.

All of this does seem a little hard to believe, and there's plenty more in science that begs belief: plate tectonics, quantum mechanics, the mating habits of certain animals, and on and on.

It would seem that, to believe all this science, one must possess a degree of faith. Certainly, both sets of statements are, on face value, hard to believe. But when you dig deeper into either one of them, you find rich structure and a tradition and a community that hold the pieces together. Both sets of statements, as written, do not reveal their internal consistency and deep connections to the world around us. In other words, both the Christian faith and modern science represent intellectual traditions that require study and patience to begin to appreciate with any real depth. Believing either one is not as crazy as it seems at first take.

But simply believing things, even if you believe them for perfectly good reasons, is not yet faith. "Now faith is the substance of things hoped for, the evidence of things not seen," writes the author of Hebrews (11:1). Nearly all Christian theologians at nearly all times have held that faith is not mere intellectual assent. Otherwise, how could it possibly be *evidence* of anything? Intellectual assent does not act in the world; belief is not itself an outward expression, for, as it is written, faith without works is dead (Jas. 2:17). To me, this means that faith without works is no faith at all.

Faith comprises both belief and action. Faith is *animate*. You believe in something and then you take action in accordance with your belief. Importantly, it is action, and not mere belief, that carries risk. Jesus was not executed because he believed in the kingdom of God, but because he had the audacity to usher it in. Martin Luther King Jr. was not assassinated because he believed in equality under the law, but because he took direct action in order to realize it. And countless Christians have, like King, followed in Jesus' footsteps, taking financial, professional, and personal risks for the furtherance of the kingdom of God.

Science does not normally demand such total commitment. Theories such as the big bang and evolution and relativity do not require us to commit our whole selves to them. They require only intellectual assent. But they do periodically demand more of certain people, and there are cases, some current, in which people put themselves in great danger because of their scientific beliefs. Take climate activist Greta Thunberg, for example. She receives daily death threats, not because she believes global warming is the gravest peril facing humanity but because she has taken concrete steps and inspired millions of people to change the system. No one cares what you believe, but many people care very much if you start acting in accordance with your beliefs, whether that belief is religious or not. Such a combination of belief and action comes close to the essence of faith, but it is rare in the scientific world.

But even this is not the same as faith in the Christian sense. The Greek word for faith is *pistis*, which carries meanings not only of belief, which we have already covered, but also of faithfulness and trust. These last words hint at the true qualitative difference between Christian belief and action and scientific belief and action: the object of belief.

What is the object of scientific belief? Ideas, theories, concepts. What is the object of Christian belief? The person of Jesus Christ. You cannot be faithful to a theory, but you can be faithful to a person. I do not know what it means to trust a theory, but I do know what it means to trust a person. The simple point I'm trying to make is, true faith requires your whole person—heart, soul, mind, and strength—precisely because it is faith in a *person*. But believing certain scientific theories requires only your mind. You may act on them, as Thunberg does, but this action is not *required* of you by the object of your belief.

Faith, in the full Christian sense of the word, demands everything you have and everything you are. This is what Jesus meant when he said that to be his followers, we are to take up our crosses daily and follow him. Science makes no such demand.

This is reflected in language used by scientists. You will almost never hear a scientist say they "believe in" the big bang theory or evolution or any other theory. Instead, they will say something such as, "I find the big bang theory to be the best scientific theory we have about the origin and evolution of the universe." This language carefully cuts out all personal aspects, a move characteristic of science itself. So, within the question, "Doesn't it take faith to believe in science?" lurks a hint of the answer, which is "no."

Question 23
Who is your favorite scientist?

For years I have admired astronomer Johannes Kepler (1571–1630). Born in Weil der Stadt, Germany, and raised in the Lutheran Church, he had intended to become a Lutheran minister. But when his scientific work began to show promise, he wrote an elated letter to his former professor, saying, "Just as I pledged myself to God, so my intention remains. I wished to be a theologian, and for a while I was anguished. But behold, now God—who wants to be known from the Book of Nature—is glorified also in astronomy through my work."*

Kepler's theology and science were blended in a way unseen in virtually any other scientist before or since. This is not to say he was always right; his earliest model of the universe, in which his Trinitarian theology was evident and played a large role, was utterly, thoroughly wrong. But his insistence on the harmony of science and faith led him beyond these wrong ideas toward one of the most astounding achievements in the history of science.

Kepler expressed his foundational belief when he wrote, "The laws [of nature] are within the grasp of the human mind; God wanted us to recognize them by creating us after his own image so that we could share in his own thoughts." He believed that the world was rational, that his scientific work expressed the divine image within him, and that he drew close to God through astronomy. Far from being a stumbling block or a threat or a problem, Kepler's science opened the very door to communion with God.

But virtually all his contemporaries disagreed. You may have difficulty imagining how radical it was, in the early 17th century, to believe that the earth revolves around the sun. Today we accept this idea easily. Your 2nd grade teacher probably told you it's true, your parents didn't fight it, and NASA says it's true. So, you believe this particular idea because the authorities say it's true. But what evidence do you have? The answer is that, unless you are a scientist in a narrowly specialized field called astrometry, you have never actually seen any material evidence that the earth moves around the sun.

In early 17th-century Europe, the situation was far more difficult. All the universities, along with the church, lined up with Aristotle when it came to questions of the earth, sun, and cosmos. The great philosopher had written that the earth stands still and that the planets—which included the sun and moon—moved around it. Importantly, this was not just an isolated fact; it affected everything. Aristotle's cosmology was foundational not only to the philosophy of the day but also to theology. Science, philosophy, and theology were so tightly connected that any rearrangement of the heavens demanded a rearrangement of all conventional

---

Johannes Kepler. Gesammelte Werke, ed. Max Caspar, et. al. (C.H. Beck, 1938) 18, 2.

thought, academic and theological, and resistance to such a rearrangement was thoroughly baked into the major institutions of the age.

So when, in 1609, Kepler published his first successful theory stating that the sun resides at the center of the cosmic arrangement, no one believed him. It was widely held that Copernicus, who had published his sun-centered theory 66 years earlier, had been wrong. Very few European astronomers agreed with Kepler, but one of them was more famous than him. In fact, it was someone you have certainly heard of: Galileo Galilei.

Galileo's support of Copernicus got him into hot water with the Catholic Church, but Kepler had his own trouble with the Lutherans. In fact, he was denied posts at Lutheran universities, due to his scientific convictions, and was even excommunicated by the Lutheran Church for his theological convictions.

This made life very difficult for Kepler. During the last half of his life, Europe was in the midst of the Thirty Years' War. Central Europe was fractured into dozens of warring Catholic and Protestant regions. As a Protestant, Kepler could not live and work in Catholic cities. And as an excommunicated Lutheran, he could not live peacefully in Protestant ones. So, welcome nowhere, he and his family were forced into a strange liminal existence, moving often and making few friends along the way. But Kepler caught a break in 1600, when he joined the team of one of the foremost astronomers of the day, Tycho Brahe.

Brahe needed the great mathematician as an assistant, but he really wanted Kepler to help him prove his own pet model of the universe, which agreed with neither Copernicus nor Aristotle. But instead of using Brahe's observational data to prove him correct, Kepler took it and showed once and for all that Copernicus had been right.

The work took years. He covered many hundreds of folio pages in mathematics and geometric diagrams, looking to make sense of the data Brahe had given him. It is difficult to imagine how far out on a limb Kepler went, working at the fringes of a far-out theory, taking seriously what nearly everyone else in the world thought was a joke, believing in the rationality of the world, and, most fundamentally, in the goodness of a God who speaks to us through pattern and order and mathematical harmony.

Sometimes the one who has his ear tuned most carefully to the voice of God rejects what everyone else values, and Kepler was no exception. In his insistence that God's truth could be found deep within Brahe's data, Kepler jettisoned two pillars of astronomical science. First was the idea that planets move at constant speed. This axiom of Aristotle went unquestioned by astronomers for nearly 2,000 years, as did another: the idea that planets must move along circular paths. Like a prophet who rejects the assumptions and values of the day in favor of a new, higher vision, Kepler dismissed these axioms out of a conviction that God was trying to tell him something—something no one else was ready to hear. He was laughed at by nearly everyone.

But his openness to new things and his insistence that God does not deceive led Kepler to scientific triumph with the publication of *Astronomia nova* in 1609. This work contained the first two of Kepler's three so-called laws of planetary motion. These are the first physical laws in the modern sense, being precise, universal, and falsifiable. They, and the planetary model they support, were sufficient to prove to the world that Copernicus had been right all along.

We normally think of Galileo, not Kepler, as the one who overturned the old idea of an earth-centered universe. It was Galileo who turned the telescope to the heavens and proved that the earth goes around the sun, not Kepler. Right? Well, maybe...

Galileo certainly was a brilliant observer, and his observations clearly showed that things in the heavens were not as they had always seemed, but he never could prove that the earth goes around the sun (and his detractors knew it). In other words, Galileo popularized Copernican astronomy: he did not prove it. But Kepler's work, abstruse as it was, was sufficient to turn the tide. Its predictions were so precise and, over the subsequent years, matched observations so well that it proved Copernicus' model in a way that Galileo's work never could.

There is much more to say about Kepler. He wrote the world's first science fiction story (*Somnium*). He insisted, against all prevailing belief, that the motions of the planets could be understood physically and not just mathematically.

He saw more than his share of hardship. He was frail and weak-eyed his whole life. He defended his mother during her witch trial (she was not a witch; the charges were trumped-up). He lost a wife and four children to disease. He was chased from town to town by the Counter Reformation. He was chronically underpaid for his work, and he never saw much of the money that was due him. He cast horoscopes to survive, yet knew they were nonsense.

In spite of all this, he never failed to see God shining through the universe; his last major publication was called *The Harmony of the World*. Yes, Johannes Kepler remains, after all these years, by far my favorite scientist.

Question 24

*What do you mean by the expression that
"wonder lies at the root of religion and science"?*

Science and faith issues often seem remote and disconnected from everyday life. I have regularly encountered people who don't see why theories such as evolution and the big bang matter when there is so much political and religious and social strife, when a pandemic is raging, when the poor are getting poorer, when so many urgent issues press down hard on us all. How does the age of the universe or the physical origin of life matter in a world crying out for peace and justice?

In a certain narrow sense, they don't. Let scientists come up with whatever theory they like: If God ever loved us, God will love us still. If Jesus ever mattered, he will matter still. If justice and reconciliation and peacemaking were ever our calling, they will be our calling still.

But Christianity is not only about peace and justice. Nor is it only about love. It is also about encountering God, who makes peace and justice possible, who is love. We share stories of such encounters with our Jewish neighbors; chief among them may be the one that tells of Moses meeting God at the burning bush, standing on holy ground in the wilderness of Sinai. It was this divine encounter that made the deliverance of Israel possible. Such meetings with God are echoed in New Testament stories such as the Transfiguration, and out of them always come redemption and new life.

These encounters with God need not be spectacular. Do not let the luminosity of the burning bush and the Transfiguration distract you from the fact that meetings with God may be small and readily available. Doors to heaven may open anywhere.

For me, science opens just such a door and invites me to meet God. All the scientific work I have ever done, from nuclear physics to astronomy, points to an evolving creation so far beyond imagining that it had to be discovered—it could never have been invented. Every time I have made a discovery, no matter how small or inconsequential, it has engendered in me a profound respect for creation, and therefore of the Creator. It has made me believe that, in living within our cosmos, we are living within a cathedral. Science and faith are, for me, absolutely inseparable.

You don't have to be a professional scientist to experience what I'm talking about; you just have to open your eyes. Discoveries need not be publishable or even original to be significant, and they are definitely not reserved for professionals.

Nearly every day of the last several years I have looked outside my window and seen a white-breasted nuthatch. On the days I haven't seen one I've heard one, soft honks coming from the oaks in my backyard or from the hickories surrounding the observatory or from the maples along the creek. Dozens of times I have stopped to watch them at the feeder outside my home office as they latch on in their funny upside-down way, select a seed, and return to their tree branch to crack and eat it or perhaps to cache it away in some tiny hiding place known only to them. From two feet away I have seen them fan their tails and spread their wings and do a little twisty dance to ward off competitors at the feeder. Black and white and blue-gray with buffy flanks, they are handsome, formal-looking birds, and their quiet voices round them off perfectly. I know few birds more intimately than I know the white-breasted nuthatch.

One day I was sitting in the kitchen and casually leafing through my copy of the *Sibley Guide to Birds,* the standard field guide. I opened it to the entry on the white-breasted nuthatch. I looked and noticed something I had not seen before: the species is sexually dimorphic. This is a scientific way of saying you can distinguish the sex of the bird by simple observation. The males and females look different from each other.

This surprised me so much I nearly passed out. I love watching birds. I take pride in noting their behavior and migration cycles, and in looking closely at the birds themselves. Over time I have come to know details of many species, details that might elude the casual observer. I can distinguish a purple finch from a house finch, a savannah sparrow from a song sparrow, a northern waterthrush from a Louisiana waterthrush, and so on. Many birders have skills that far outstrip my own, of course, but I know a little about local bird life.

So, when I discovered that white-breasted nuthatch males can easily be distinguished from white-breasted nuthatch females, I was floored. This is a bird I thought I knew! Granted, it's not the most obvious difference; the bird's cap is much darker and more extensive in the male, and his colors are more vibrant. But when I looked back over some photographs I had taken, I found that both males and females regularly visited our feeder, and I can now see clearly who is who. It was there all along, hidden in plain sight.

This business of the white-breasted nuthatch once again put me in awe of a Creator who offers more beauty and surprises on a daily basis than I could sort through in a lifetime. It made me feel humble, grateful, awed, and respectful of this world God so loves.

Creation is open to you too, just waiting for you to discover it. Go and observe, and, as you do, please remember that the simple, familiar activities of nature-watching—observation and classification—are fully scientific. The fact that such observations and classifications have been made and documented by others makes them no less scientific. When you look at the world—really look at it and engage it and think about it—you are doing science. Scientists just happen to be people who have found a way to make a living doing this.

The Babylonian Talmud tells of the death of one Rabbi Eliezer. His devoted students stood around his deathbed and pleaded for him to share his life's wisdom so that they may lead fulfilling lives and enter the world to come. The rabbi said something about mutual respect, something about raising their future children, and concluded by saying, "When you pray, know before whom you stand."

Know before whom you stand. The Rabbi's words are found in synagogues throughout the world, where they are inscribed above the ark that holds the Torah. They point to the essential stance we must have when we turn to meet God: humility, reverence, awe, gratitude.

If, as you turn to observe the world outside your window, or at your local park, or in the night sky, you pray and know before whom you stand, your wonder will be rewarded not only with a small bit of knowledge of and appreciation for creation, but also an encounter with the Creator.

Question 25
What is your favorite faith-and-science passage in the Bible?

In a certain narrow sense, I don't have a favorite faith-and-science passage because there really is no science in the Bible. What we today call "science" did not appear until more than a thousand years after the biblical canon was established. However ancient Israel may have approached the created world, they did not perform controlled experiments or make systematic, quantitative observations of nature with the purpose of understanding how it works.

We would be in business, however, if you were to rephrase your question to "What is your favorite passage about creation in the Bible?" The word "creation" implies the presence of a creator, and scripture is saturated with the theme of creation.

In response to the creation question, then, I have a lot to think about. You cannot beat Genesis 1 for its liturgical grandeur; Genesis 2 for its messy, down-to-earth, improvisational character; or Isaiah 40–66 for its rhapsodic vision of a new creation. Proverbs 8:22-31 celebrates the foundational role of wisdom in the creation of the world, and Psalm 104 praises God for all creatures—even the great sea monster Leviathan. And Job 38–41 takes us on an unforgettable tour of a brilliant and brutal cosmos.

But for sheer efficiency and scope, for drawing together the human and the cosmic, for inviting us into a coherent and morally serious view of the cosmos and us in it, one can do no better than Ps. 19:1-10.

> The heavens are telling the glory of God; and the firmament proclaims his handiwork. Day to day pours forth speech, and night to night declares knowledge. There is no speech, nor are there words; their voice is not heard; yet their voice goes out through all the earth, and their words to the end of the world. In the heavens he has set a tent for the sun, which comes out like a bridegroom from his wedding canopy, and like a strong man runs its course with joy. Its rising is from the end of the heavens, and its circuit to the end of them; and nothing is hidden from its heat. The law of the Lord is perfect, reviving the soul; the decrees of the Lord are sure, making wise the simple; the precepts of the Lord are right, rejoicing the heart; the commandment of the Lord is clear, enlightening the eyes; the fear of the Lord is pure, enduring for ever; the ordinances of the Lord are true and righteous altogether. More to be desired are they than gold, even much fine gold; sweeter also than honey, and drippings of the honeycomb.

We often think of human beings as separate from creation; values such as wisdom and justice and righteousness seem to have nothing to do with the universe, and the universe seems to have nothing to do with them. The ancient and evolving biophysical world is surely disconnected from, indifferent to, and perhaps even hostile to the moral imperatives so central to our lives as humans. In the face of this uniquely modern problem, Psalm 19 invites us to behold the cosmos anew, as a coherent, unified whole.

The first four verses emphasize creation. David, the traditional author of this psalm, seems to be in a playful mood. The heavens declare, he writes. They proclaim, they speak with a clear voice. At the same time there is no speech, no voice, no words. How can this be? A riddle has been posed to us.

I believe we all know the answer to this riddle, especially those of us who sense a deep attraction to the created world. Creation speaks and never ceases, not for a day, not for a night, not for a minute.

The psalmist looks to the heavens as an example, and it is an excellent one. As a professional astronomer who has spent a lot of time thinking about and looking at the night sky, I can say that I have, upon gazing skyward, heard this voiceless voice.

But, of course, the sky turns for everyone, and viewing it is free. Everyone gets the same stars, the same planets, the same sun and moon. And they speak to all people without ceasing, day and night. But if the heavens declare, what do they say?

They say something about beauty. Beauty, as art critic Sister Wendy Beckett reminds us, is not a pretty word; it is a strong word. The beauty of the heavens, like the heavens themselves, reveals something fundamental, something concrete.

The heavens say that reality transcends our most daring thoughts. They suggest that there may be more intelligent life in the universe than mere *Homo sapiens*. They tell us that creation is not only orderly but also wildly, fabulously creative. They proclaim knowledge, suggestive of physical laws that we have begun to understand today but that the author of Psalm 19 could not have imagined.

Verses 5-6 introduce a variation on the cosmic theme. To 21st-century readers this new theme is hidden, but it is nonetheless present behind the words as the psalmist praises the sun in the figures of bridegroom and running man.

These lines almost certainly have their inspiration in the broader context of the ancient Near East, a context in which the sun was considered to be the god of law and justice. This is not to say our author considers the sun to be a god—one of the interesting things about ancient Israel is that they did *not* consider the moon and stars and sun to be gods—but rather that the connection between the sun and law and justice was in the air, so to speak, and so shows up here.

And next we see why. These sun-law-justice verses transition the reader between the first section and the second, in which the author's focus switches explicitly from creation to the moral law, which rejoices the heart and enlightens the eyes. At this point the psalm sounds exactly like Proverbs, that great storehouse of traditional wisdom. Even the fear of the Lord, perhaps the most prominent theme of the book of Proverbs, is emphasized.

Unlike creation, the law praised by the psalmist—the Ten Commandments plus all the additional laws of the Pentateuch—concerns human beings directly. It provides a roadmap for creating a good, useful, beautiful, and righteous life. Righteousness is just a stained-glass word for justice, of course, so the law bears both individual and communal elements. The law tells us how to live in this world successfully—how to live a morally serious life, how to show love to others, how to get along.

So, stepping back, we see two themes: creation, which declares knowledge; and the moral law, which enlightens the eyes. Is the author simply saying that both creation and the law are good and beautiful and praiseworthy and thus go together nicely?

No. More is happening here, and again we miss it if we fail to understand the cosmology of ancient Israel. Creation, in this view, is not just organized elements, the law is not just words in a book, and justice is not just something people achieve. A deep, powerful reality animates both creation and the moral law and binds them together in a single vision. This reality is called "wisdom."

Wisdom is alive, dynamic, creative, and cosmic. Wisdom was present at the time of creation (Proverbs 8) and is best understood as an attribute of God folded into the fabric of all things, human and nonhuman alike. Law, justice, beauty, creativity, and knowledge are all grounded in wisdom, which shines through all creation and remains accessible to all people everywhere for the building up of righteous lives and justice-filled communities.

By singing praises to God for creation and the moral law in a single hymn, the author of Psalm 19 weaves all the elements of the universe into a unified cosmic tapestry. Through both creation and human morality, God calls us to choose wisdom, to stitch our own lives into this tapestry, to take part in it, to become part of it.

There is a unity and coherence to this view, at once particular and universal, that attracts us 21st-century folks and that helps us draw together all the elements of our often-fragmented worlds.

Question 26
There is much in the Bible about heaven and earth, but isn't Mars cool too?

Yes, it is! And since Mars is one of the five planets human beings can see with their unaided vision, and one of the brightest of these, it has drawn our interest since before recorded history. We have not only studied Mars with telescopes and landers and rovers, but we have also written poems about it, told stories about it, and even given it a personality. Mars challenges our intellects and excites our imaginations.

So, it comes as no surprise that so many people have been fascinated by our most recent mission to Mars. In February, 2021, after a 6.5-month journey from Earth, the *Perseverance Rover* touched down and began operations on the surface of Mars. NASA scientists chose Jezero Crater, just north of the Martian equator, as the landing site for *Perseverance*. The reason for this choice is simple: Billions of years ago, Jezero and the surrounding area were once flooded with water. In fact, billions of years ago, Jezero was the location of an ancient river delta.

Yes, Mars once had liquid water on its surface, and its northern hemisphere may have been entirely covered by a vast ocean. Like all planets, Mars was much warmer long ago. It has since cooled considerably, just as Earth and the other planets have, and today Mars is too cold to support standing water on its surface; its average temperature is about −70°F. But back in the early days of the solar system, water pooled and ran across the Martian surface—just as it does on Earth today.

And why is water so important? Because, as far as we can tell, liquid water is a prerequisite for life. And life is what this mission, and nearly all scientific work on Mars, is really about, and in two ways.

First, it is about alien life. In the early days of the scientific study of Mars, speculation arose about the possibility of life there. One fellow, Giovanni Schiaparelli, a 19th-century Italian astronomer, saw through his telescope details on the surface of Mars that he called "channels." When he published his findings, the term "channels" had been translated into English as "canals." This word, unlike "channels," suggests some kind of artificial construction. This mistranslation gave rise to speculation and folklore about the possibility of intelligent life on Mars, and the term "Martians" was coined.

Among the speculators was found the prominent astronomer Percival Lowell, who spent much of his career championing the idea of intelligent life on Mars. And while he did succeed in discovering Pluto, he was quite wrong about the Martians. But the idea of canals on Mars remained fixed in the public imagination, as did the terribly exciting notion of Martians. Throughout the 20th century, storytellers and science fiction writers mined the deep and widespread notion of life on Mars in their quest to entertain and enlighten people. The 1938 *War of the Worlds* radio broadcast scare, in which some listeners came to believe that Martians had actually invaded New York City, stands as a prime example of this trend.

Today, thanks to a number of landers and rovers equipped with cameras and scientific equipment, we have observed Mars up close and have encountered no direct evidence of life, past or present, intelligent or otherwise. But we still have a lot of looking to do: one piece of the *Perseverance* mission is to search the ancient river delta for signs of life.

A second piece of the *Perseverance* mission also has to do with life, but not alien life—human life. Human beings have long dreamed of traveling to and colonizing other planets, and, however it plays out, Mars will definitely be our first stop. Some features of Mars make it a very attractive target: it's close, its day is only 37 minutes longer than ours, and it has seasons as does Earth.

But the similarities end there. Getting to Mars and back will be a triumph of technology, grit, and know-how. But remaining on Mars for any length of time will be much more difficult for several reasons:

- Gravity is much feebler than on Earth, so after some time on Mars our bones and muscles will grow weak (and this process may not be reversible).
- Because the average temperature is extremely low, outdoor activities won't be possible without heavy suits.
- The atmosphere is composed almost entirely of carbon dioxide and contains only a trace of oxygen, so there's no way we could breathe it.
- The thin air allows lots of ultraviolet light to reach the surface so cancer, cognitive disease, and reproductive problems will multiply.
- The planet lacks a magnetic field, so it's constantly bombarded with fast-moving electrons and protons from the sun—which means even more cancer.
- Mars orbits further from the sun than Earth, so even bright days will seem dim.
- Because of its distance from the sun and the lack of surface water and organics in the soil, it will be impossible to grow food or anything else.
- No germs live on Mars, so our immune systems will lose their ability to fight any diseases that may arrive on spaceships from Earth.

Other challenges abound, but these points serve to make my case: colonizing Mars will be hard to do.

But human beings are nothing if not ingenious and hard-working, and *Perseverance* has recently shown that it is possible to extract oxygen from the atmospheric carbon dioxide. This oxygen not only can be breathed by visiting astronauts and possible future colonists, but also can be used to power rockets leaving the Martian surface.

Speaking of the surface, the Red Planet is well named. Its color is caused by the iron in the surface rocks combining with the oxygen in the planet's atmosphere, which produces iron oxide. We earthlings have another name for iron oxide: rust. Yes, that's right: the surface of Mars is literally rusting away, and this rust gives it a distinct ruddy glow when seen against the dark night sky.

The question naturally arises: Why would we spend so much money and employ thousands of scientists and engineers and commit so many years of hard effort to leave our rich green world, flowing with water and filled with life, in favor of a rusty, cold, apparently-dead hazard of a planet such as Mars?

Many answers arise in response to this question. Some have to do with the nature of human beings, how we relentlessly explore and ask questions. Other answers have to do with politics, and some with economics. But the Christian has a different set of challenges: Why, in a world so filled with need, so crowded with the least of these, should we turn our eyes upward and dream of visiting a red light in the sky?

But this is not an either/or question. The two impulses—serving others and exploring the solar system, which is our home—are not set in natural opposition. They are not mutually exclusive. In fact, any success we may have in space exploration will be a sign of our care for others. Any society that does not lift up and care for and educate all its people will have neither the human resources nor the spirit required to go where no man or woman has gone before.

But if we do follow Jesus' command to love, to search out the lost, to bring hope to the poor, and to serve one another, we will find one day that traveling to Mars is not only possible but also inevitable.

Question 27
Should Christians trust scientists?

During the long months of the COVID-19 pandemic in America, it has become obvious that many people still refuse to be vaccinated. A surprisingly large fraction of these are Christians. In 2021 the Pew Research Center conducted a survey and found that white evangelicals are the religious group least likely to say they would receive the COVID-19 vaccination. Nearly half (45%) said they would not get the shot, compared with 30% of the general population.

"We are creations of God and we will follow Him and we will do as He has called us to do," said Orlando resident Holly Meade, adding that she was exercising her religious freedom and trusting in God for her health.[1] "We're anti-mask, anti-social distancing, and anti-vaccine," said Tony Spell, a minister at the Life Tabernacle Church in Baton Rouge, La.[2] He believed the vaccine was politically motivated, and used his pulpit to discourage church members from taking the vaccine.

Perhaps Meade and Spell and others like them have a point. It seems that Christians should not trust scientists. Few scientists are Christians, after all: Why should we trust those outside our fold? Why should we, who claim to have access to the truth about the world, rely on those who do not?

Proverbs 3:5 directs us to "Trust in the Lord with all your heart and lean not on your own understanding." And what is science if not our own human understanding? Perhaps science is a product of human pride and a show of independence from God. It does not require any reference to God or scripture or theology; it operates completely outside anything we might call "trust in the Lord." Human beings, left in this way to our own skills and devices, always fall short of the goal. If we could ground science in scripture, then perhaps we could think of scientists as trustworthy. But as it is, we should regard them and their statements with skepticism.

Moreover, this world is passing away. As Christians we are citizens of another, more real, spiritual world. Even if science were grounded in scripture, we should place no true hope in it, for even our best understanding of the Bible and even our best theology are written and apprehended through a glass darkly. Nothing but Jesus on this side of heaven can be relied on. Therefore science, established as it is in this present darkness, is tainted at the source.

Finally, science has again and again challenged traditional religious views of creation and human identity. Evolution by natural selection, for example, throws a skeptical light on the creation story found in Genesis, brings into question the notion of human specialness, and paints a picture not of a blessed and very good creation but of millions of years of brutal and bloody struggle for survival and dominance. Certain cosmological and neuroscientific theories cast doubt on the veracity of the Bible and the special status of human beings. More could be said about this but, in general, science has proven itself to be not merely neutral but actually antagonistic toward belief.

On the contrary, however, when, in Matthew 22, the lawyer asks Jesus to name the greatest commandment, Jesus responds: "You shall love the Lord your God with all your heart, and with all your soul, and with all your mind." This story, including the piece about loving God with all your mind, occurs also in Mark and Luke. Jesus' words cannot be ignored or brushed away. When Jesus is directly asked what is most important in life, he not only does what he almost never does—give an immediate and clear answer—but he also includes in his answer an imperative to engage our minds, granting them the same status as our hearts and souls. I conclude that there is such a thing as the intellectual love of God, and that to reject the full and honest use of our minds is to disobey the central commandment of our faith.

Genesis 1:26-28 tells us that human beings are made in the image of God. Jewish and Christian scholars have debated the meaning of this phrase—the image of God—for thousands of years, and many suggestions have been made as to what it might signify. Some have said our use of symbolic language makes us like God; others have pointed to our capacity for love, or to our drive to create. Still others have suggested that we are most similar to God in the use of our minds, in our ability to think and to think about our thinking. So, without insisting that this be the whole of the divine image, I believe we can say that in using our minds we reflect something of God's nature, just as we do in the full exercise of our hearts and souls.

And what is science if not the use of our minds? If we reject science, then we reject the direct and first commandment of Jesus, who tells us to love God with *all* of our minds, including the scientific parts. Further, I say that loving creation is necessarily a part of loving the Creator. Who, if given the gift of a painting from their beloved, would not love the painting as part of the greater love? Moreover, if we reject science, we also reject the fruits of those who, wittingly or not, have obeyed the same commandment.

If science had been a historical disaster, we would have warrant to reject it. But the overall fruitfulness of science only adds weight to my response. I hardly need to enumerate here the many ways science has benefited us (notably by vaccines), nor do I need to convince you that science tends, over time, to work. It does not do all things: it cannot tell us how to live, nor is it intended to replace theology or ethics or philosophy. But its success within its own domain signifies that science tells us something real about the world God so loves.

Therefore, I answer that, in light of the greatest and first commandment and of the historical success of the scientific enterprise, Christians should trust science and scientists. Now to object to my first three arguments:

As to the statement that Christians should not trust those who are not Christians… every human being carries the divine image. Hence, it is not necessary to be Christian to be moral, or loving, or correct, or to have deep insight about the human situation or about creation. To refuse to be influenced by non-Christians is not only shortsighted but also impossible. So far as we have control over it, which may not be very far, the question is not whether to allow ourselves to be affected by nonbelievers; it is about what and to what ends shall we be so affected.

As to the statement about this world passing away… on one level it seems to be true: the earth will not last forever. Yet ours is precisely the world God so loved that he sent his only begotten son. We are not here by accident, nor is the world a waiting room or some kind of triage. It is the very good creation of God, and we are each a part of it and are to live out our days in hope and fidelity, loving God with all our heart, soul, and mind and loving one another as ourselves.

As to the statement that science challenges certain traditional Christian beliefs… this is true. The cosmos that scientists have revealed often forces us back to the theological drawing board. We must rethink not only the nature of creation, humanity, and God, but also the way the three relate. Where does the Adam-and-Eve story fit on a geologic timeline? Are humans merely products of blind, impersonal forces such as natural selection? How does Jesus fit into a 13.8-billion-year-old evolving cosmos? Where, in such a universe, is there a place for a creator? If our brains are essentially extraordinarily complex electric computers, where does that leave the soul? If we can be protected by a vaccine, what use is there for prayer?

But it is precisely these questions to which the greatest and first commandment draws us. To love God with all our heart, soul, and mind means that we should not run from the unknown nor fear answers we don't prefer, but instead to work courageously toward understanding the world. Because for this scientist at least, that's what the loving God looks like.

Notes

[1] www.wesh.com/article/religion-and-the-covid-19-vaccine/36327359#.

[2] www.dw.com/en/american-evangelicals-and-the-resistance-to-covid-vaccines/a-55957915.

Question 28
What is meant by the universe being "finely tuned" for the existence of life?

Numbers describe certain aspects of the universe with uncanny precision. This should come as no surprise to anyone who has taken a class in physical science. The fields of chemistry, geology, and biology contain heavily quantitative subfields. Medical professionals deal with numbers all the time, as do sociologists and anthropologists. But the field of physics assigns mathematics a more central and profound role than any other science.

Galileo explored the mathematical nature of the physical world more deeply than anyone before him, and Johannes Kepler, Galileo's contemporary, proposed the first true mathematical natural laws. Since then, physicists have discovered no limits to the mathematical structure of the universe. When Einstein wrote that the single most incomprehensible thing about the universe is that it is comprehensible, he was referring largely to mathematics, and the idea that mathematics saturates the cosmos remains a bedrock idea of all the physical sciences.

Cosmology, the branch of astrophysics that explores the universe on its largest scales of space and time, is full of staggering numbers. Some boggle the mind not because of their large or small values, but because of their scientific and philosophical implications.

In 1999 Sir Martin Rees, former Master of Trinity College of Cambridge University and the United Kingdom's Astronomer Royal, wrote a book titled *Just Six Numbers*. In this short and conversational volume, Rees lays out a simple but astonishing idea: the large-scale structure of the universe is governed by just six numbers, and if any of these six numbers differed even slightly, life as we know it would not be possible. What's more, these numbers seem to be independent of each other, so any of them could be different than they are without affecting the others.

Imagine that you are the master chef of the cosmic kitchen. In front of you stands an oven. This oven is used not for baking casseroles or cookies but for baking universes. It is controlled by six dials and a single large button. Each dial controls one of Rees' six numbers, and your job is to bake a universe in which life can exist. The recipe consists of just six numbers. Which ones do you pick?

The first dial is labeled N and allows you to control the relative strengths of two of the fundamental forces that act in your universe. If N is less than the number 1, gravity is stronger than the electromagnetic force; if N is greater than 1, the electromagnetic force is stronger than gravity.

You dial up a value of 10^{36}, which is a short way of writing the number 1 followed by 36 zeros. So, your electromagnetic force is incomprehensibly stronger than gravity. But this is the number you must choose, for if N were just slightly smaller, stars would burn their fuel at a higher rate and have much shorter lifetimes. They would not persist for the billions of years required for life to evolve.

The second dial controls the factor Ω, which controls the density of your universe. For a life-supporting cosmos, you must set this number very close to 1. If you set its value lower, stars and galaxies will never form; if you set it higher, the universe will collapse back on itself shortly after you press the BAKE button—again not persisting long enough for life to develop.

The third dial is marked D. It allows you to determine the number of spatial dimensions in your universe. You may be surprised that you have the option to choose 2 or 4 or 5 or any other number of dimensions, but you do. It's your kitchen! But if you don't choose 3, then all kinds of barriers to life will show up, one of them being that the orbits of planets and moons will not be stable. And life needs a nice, stable environment in which to flourish, so you pick $D=3$.

The fourth dial is marked with the letter Q, and this one adjusts the rest energy of matter to the strength of, again, the gravitational force. The details do not concern us, but for life to be possible in your universe you must set the value of Q to be about 100,000. If it were a little smaller, star formation would be very slow and the raw material needed to build up planets would not survive long enough to do so. If Q were a little larger, the universe would not be populated by many billions of bright stars but by many billions of black holes. In both cases your universe would be lifeless.

You use the fifth dial to adjust something called "nuclear efficiency," represented by ε, the Greek letter epsilon. It tells you how easily light elements such as hydrogen and helium combine to make heavier ones such as carbon and oxygen. The smaller this number, the easier it is to sustain nuclear fusion in stellar cores; the higher this number, the harder. If you want life in your universe, you must set $\varepsilon=0.007$. If you turn it down to 0.006, there will never be elements other than hydrogen in your universe; if you turn it up to 0.008, all hydrogen will be immediately converted into heavy elements and there would be none left over to power stars or create water.

The final dial on your oven is called the "cosmological constant Λ" which measures a kind of anti-gravity effect. Einstein worked this parameter into his equations in his theory of general relativity, but later believed that doing so constituted the worst blunder of his career. But now scientists think he may have been onto something after all. In the actual universe, Λ clocks in at a remotely tiny value—122 zeros after a decimal point, followed by a 1—and if it were to exceed this value by much, then there probably would be no stars or galaxies at all, and again, no life.

So, if you want to bake a universe in which life is even possible, your six dials must be carefully set to the values we find in the actual universe. Some have more flexibility than others, but you, as the master chef, are very tightly constrained. You can have four dimensions. You can have a universe in which the gravitational force is stronger than the electromagnetic. You can have a universe with stars that burn hydrogen rapidly. You can have a super dense universe. But you can't have any of these *and* life too.

This fact—that the actual universe seems to be finely tuned for life—has been lifted up as evidence for God by some scientists and philosophers. Others have countered by pointing out that, if the universe were not fit for life, we would not be here to talk about it. The skeptics are of course logically correct, and there are other reasons to be wary of rushing to a supernatural conclusion. For example, we do not yet know why these numbers have the values they do, and the day may come when we see that they are not independent. We may come to understand that they could not in fact be other than they are. Furthermore, perhaps our understanding of life is too provincial, too earth-centered. It seems possible that alien creatures could thrive in circumstances far beyond what we have yet imagined, including in some of the universes we have written off as incompatible with life. So perhaps the God conclusion is premature. Maybe, as scientists like to say, we need more data.

But for myself, I do find some significance in these six numbers. I am surprised and happy that life seems to have missed oblivion by the narrowest of margins. It is like standing against a wall, blindfolded and faced by a six-member firing squad on a clear windless day. Then the unthinkable happens: The shots ring out, but every bullet misses you. Now the probability of such an event is vanishingly small, but not zero, and it seems you have simply drawn the most improbable card ever. If you hadn't, you wouldn't be around to know it. Even so, as you walk away you involuntarily look up at heaven and ask: Why am I still alive?

Question 29
*How do faith and science come together for you in your
daily practice of the Christian life?*

As a physics professor and minister, I am always moving between the college and the church, between the science building and the sanctuary. I have "physics days," and I have "Jesus days." But I do not contain two distinct, separate halves. I have no hard, analytical half that awakens on physics days while my softer, more loving half snoozes. I have no compassionate, pastoral half that shows up on Jesus days while my fact-happy half takes the day off. Faith and science intersect in my life all the time, every day.

To explain one way this happens, I'd like to tell you about a fellow named Samuel Hubbard Scudder, an entomologist who worked in the late 19th and early 20th centuries. In his 1874 essay titled, "Learning to See," he tells a humorous story of his first interactions with perhaps the greatest American scientist of the time, zoologist Luis Agassiz, at Harvard University.*

Scudder was a newly-enrolled graduate student and wished to work under Agassiz. He entered the great professor's office and told him of his plans. After a short chat Agassiz agreed and asked, "When would you like to start?" Scudder replied, "Now."

Pleased, Agassiz reached into a jar of alcohol, pulled out a dead fish, and laid it in a tray before Scudder. "Now look at this fish," he said, "and in a little while I will ask you what you have seen." Scudder was to use only his hands and eyes. Optical instruments such as magnifying glasses were forbidden. The professor left the aspiring scientist alone with the very ordinary and very dead fish.

"In 10 minutes I had seen all there was to see in that fish," wrote Scudder. He stood up and began searching for the professor, but he was not to be found. Unsettled but not knowing what else to do, Scudder returned to the fish and spent the rest of the morning investigating it, picking it up, looking at it from every angle, poking his finger down its throat, even counting the scales at one point. After some time, he began to find the fish loathsome.

Noon arrived and Agassiz had still not returned, so Scudder placed the creature in its jar and went to lunch, smelling of fish and yellow alcohol. When he returned to the lab after an hour, he was told that the professor had been there but had gone for the afternoon. So, Scudder devoted two more hours to the fish. He had just started drawing it when Agassiz walked in.

"Well, what is the fish like?" Agassiz asked. He then listened as Scudder outlined what he fancied was a rather detailed description of the fish's gills, eyes, lips, fins, teeth, tail, and so forth, based on Scudder's several hours of observation.

*Scudder's story can be found in several places online, including emu.edu/writing-program/docs/Scudder.pdf.

"You have not looked very carefully," Agassiz said with obvious disappointment. "Look again!"

Scudder, desperate now, returned to the fish, which at this point he described as "hideous." After a few more hours he spoke again with Agassiz, who was again disappointed. "You have not seen the fish," he said. Eventually Scudder settled down and fully devoted himself to the project. In the end he spent three full days paying attention to the poor dead fish, and he never stopped discovering new things about it.

This simple act of paying attention lies at the foundation of all science, and it requires that we set aside what we think the world is like, what we'd rather be doing, and any personal agendas we might have. It requires that we open ourselves to what lies present before us.

All the scientific work I have done, from the nuclear lab to the NASA conference room to the physics classroom, requires that I pay attention: to data, to nature, to patterns. It also demands that I pay attention to colleagues and students, for the act of paying attention, so essential for scientific work, is not limited to the nonhuman world.

When I was in college, I hung out a lot in the student center. Some Baptist students discovered I was not a Christian, so they tried to turn me into one. I made an easy target, sitting there with my coffee and my physics books. It became a game. They would sit down and try to argue me into believing in God and their religious system, whatever it was, and I refused. It was fun, arguing. I could go for hours, and in the courtroom of my mind I won every argument every time.

One day a new Christian sat down with me, and I could not argue with her. Her name was Elizabeth. I could not argue with Elizabeth, and that's not because she was good at arguing. It's because she didn't *care* about arguing. She had no interest in arguing with me, so she didn't.

Instead, she paid attention to me. She played no games and attempted no sales jobs. She did not try to convert me. It was a pretty pure thing: two bright, open eyes and one bright, open mind—right across the table, looking at me through the coffee steam. I don't know if you have ever had the experience of someone really paying attention to you, out of the blue and without warning, but I can tell you it's a little disarming. It's a little baffling. It's a little bewildering. It's a little irresistible. There is no gift like the gift of one's full attention.

It was a gift because she simply offered herself to me. She had no schemes, no need to be right, no need to turn me into a Christian. She was interested in me, so she paid attention to me. In 2021, we celebrated our 30th anniversary.

When I am at church, whether teaching or leading worship or listening to a parishioner, I strive to pay attention to others in the same way Elizabeth paid attention to me. I try to love others in that same way, because to pay attention is to love.

Near the end of the Sermon on the Mount, Jesus asks us, "Why do you see the speck in your neighbor's eye, but do not notice the log in your own eye? Or how can you say to your neighbor, 'Let me take the speck out of your eye,' while the log is in your own eye? You hypocrite, first take the log out of your own eye, and then you will see clearly to take the speck out of your neighbor's eye" (Matt. 7:3-5).

On the day he walked into Professor Agassiz's office, Samuel Scudder was already a successful student of zoology. He thought he knew what a fish looked like. Maybe the log in his eye was his overconfidence, or his impatience, or his desire to impress his new mentor. Maybe he had personal plans for those three days and wanted to be done with the dead fish. But such logs only kept him from seeing what was in front of him. I try daily to remove these same logs—my ego, my desire to get on to the next thing, my need to impress other people—so that I might think clearly about science and theology.

When they tried to convert me to Christianity, my fellow students came at me with their own logs: their desire to be right, their need to win me for Christ and prop up their own view of the world, their impulse to do good. But these agendas blocked their view of who was sitting right there in front of them.

The fundamental act of both science and faith is to be present with what or who is before us, to really see them, to remove the logs from our eyes so that we may see the world clearly. The practice of paying attention is the first act of scientific inquiry and the first act of religious life, and on my good days this is a distinction without a difference.

Question 30
What is "intelligent design"?

The spectrum of beliefs regarding science and faith is divided into several categories. Intelligent design (ID) is a belief held by many people across the spectrum, and in particular by creationists. It does not comprise a new school of creationism; nor does it compete with any form of creationism. Instead, it is a broad philosophical perspective that, for its adherents, supports the general creationist point of view.

Unlike creationism, ID carries no explicit religious agenda and makes no cultural or political demands on its adherents, who consider ID to be a scientific theory. Many subscribers to ID come across with an open-minded, "come let us reason together" mindset, and ID itself does not reject evolution wholesale. It therefore appeals to creationists who value a more sophisticated and intellectual approach.

But what *is* ID? That's easy enough to say. A think tank called the Discovery Institute has acted as ID headquarters since 1991, and on its website we find this definition: "The theory of intelligent design holds that certain features of the universe and of living things are best explained by an intelligent cause, not an undirected process such as natural selection."[1]

The phrase "certain features" indicates that, for advocates of ID, some aspects of the cosmos are fully scientifically comprehensible without making recourse to an intelligent cause. Atoms may be one of these, for example. The atomic theory is understandable in terms of what one might call mainstream science, which makes no appeal to an intelligent designer. But, ID advocates say, not all features of the cosmos are like this. Some features of the universe, they claim, are scientifically incomprehensible without reference to an intelligent designer. These include specific biological details that defy explanation in terms of standard evolutionary mechanisms such as natural selection. Which details are these?

The most famous example held up by ID advocates is a fascinating mechanism known as the "bacterial flagellum," a tiny inboard-outboard motor that provides propulsion for certain cells. It features a driveshaft embedded in the cell wall. Torque is delivered by an ion-driven motor, and the shaft itself is attached—via a microscopic universal joint—to a long, whip-like propeller that extends far beyond the cell's body; the whip corkscrews and pushes the cell along. It is really an impressive device; flagella rotate at several thousand rpm and can propel bacteria up to speeds of approximately 35 cell lengths per second (compare this to the top speed of a cheetah, about 25 cheetah lengths per second). The flagellum can reverse itself within a quarter of a turn. It is a truly remarkable feature of the cosmos, perhaps the most elegant nano-machine described by science. It is so amazing, in fact, that ID advocates insist it cannot possibly have evolved via natural selection.

Why not? Because it is, to use their phrase, "irreducibly complex." This means that the flagellum requires every one of its parts—and there are many I have not mentioned—to function. Take away even the smallest, least-important-seeming part from the flagellum and it will no longer mobilize its bacterium. The oft-floated analogy is that of a mousetrap: Take away the base or the catch or the spring or the holding bar or the hammer, and it just won't work. You no longer have a mousetrap: you just have a few random parts that can do nothing in the way of trapping mice.

This irreducible complexity, so goes the ID argument, is a hallmark of things that could not have been built via natural selection, which always works piecemeal on what is already in place. Such a slow, piece-by-piece process could not have assembled, over any number of remotely tiny steps, such a mechanism as the flagellum. The mechanism must have arisen, therefore, as an "integrated unit, in one fell swoop, for natural selection to have anything to work on," writes biochemist Michael Behe, a leader in the ID movement who has written extensively on the bacterial flagellum.[2]

Adherents of ID point to other examples of irreducible complexity such as the eye and the blood-clotting cascade, both of which, admittedly, are enormously complex (and fascinating).

Irreducible complexity is not the only hallmark of intelligent design in nature, say ID supporters. Something called "specified complexity" is revealed in DNA and other features of the universe, and ID supporters say it too points to design. Specified complexity has to do with probability and information theory, and ID proponents use it to argue that the probability of life as we know it evolving out of random, undirected events is so remotely tiny as to be zero.

Other arguments are also made, but they all support the ID thesis that, since conventional science seems to be incapable of explaining some parts of the universe, these parts must have been designed. Behe writes, "It is a shock to us... to discover, from observations science has made, that the fundamental mechanisms of life cannot be ascribed to natural selection, and therefore were designed."[3]

Scientists have responded with vigor to the claims of ID and have shown it to be a scientific nonstarter. My present objection to ID, however, does not rest on its scientific details but on its fundamental logic, which admits only two possibilities: natural selection or intelligent design. This prematurely closes off all other possibilities. Many theories we accept today were undreamed-of by earlier scientists, and perhaps some as-yet unknown idea is out there waiting to be discovered. But this has ever been the case and I would not even bring it up if not for my second objection, which is this: The idea of an intelligent designer is not scientific.

Science is limited, which is one reason for its tremendous success. It is not about everything. In setting up an intelligent designer as an alternative to natural selection, ID advocates have set up a nonscientific idea as an alternative to a scientific one. This would be fine if ID were content to call itself philosophy, but it claims to be a scientific theory. It is not. In claiming evidence of an intelligent designer, it has jumped the rails of science, regardless of who the designer is. "Design" is not a scientific category, and ID proponents put too much of a burden on science when it insists otherwise.

Intelligent design is at heart a religious theory, although its key proponents, not content to let science be science, deny this. Nearly all of them are conservative Christians, but they understand that bringing God into the discussion would short-circuit their effort, which is formally aimed at scientists and skeptics. Therefore, they maintain religious neutrality by not naming the designer. They do not say who assembled the flagella or organized the DNA. All they claim, at least publicly, is that the detailed structure of these things constitutes scientific evidence for a designer.

It is easy to see how this idea appeals to creationists, who insist that life arose from specific acts of divine creation, who emphasize specific cases that appear to support their position, who look to the Bible to guide them in all these efforts, and who reject scientific arguments that threaten their understanding of scripture.

As a Christian, I do not reject the idea of a designer (although "designer" is not a term I would ever use). But Christians in general do not need to shrink from science and its naturalistic methods, because we more than others have a rich tradition in which to locate these things, a larger context that allows us to take science seriously but not too seriously.

For a person of faith, ID is not just an unnecessary choice; it is a harmful one. Like creationism itself, it reduces God to a kind of holy tinkerer. It locates the divine in places of ignorance and obscurity. And this gives it a defensive and fearful spirit that is out of place in Christian faith and theology.

Notes

[1] See www.discovery.org/id/faqs/.
[2] Michael Behe, *Darwin's Black Box* (Free Press, 1996), 39.
[3] See www.discovery.org/a/54/.

Question 31
What is the multiverse, and what does it have to do with God?

Our universe is well suited for life. It must be so, of course, because here we are to talk about it. If our universe were not well suited for life, we would not know it! But this seemingly innocent, self-evident statement has launched a long and vigorous conversation at the intersection of theology and science.

The first thing to get clear is that our universe could have been otherwise. The numbers introduced in Question 28 make the universe what it is. One of these numbers controls the rate at which stars burn hydrogen fuel; if it had a different value, then stars could not last long enough for life to evolve. Another number ensures that the universe didn't collapse back on itself a second after the big bang. A third number allows planets to maintain stable orbits, and so forth. Furthermore, these numbers do not depend on one another. They are independent. Any of them could be different without affecting the others. If any of them changed, the universe would be a very different place.

In fact, if any of the six constants had values other than they do, life as we know it would not be possible. So these six constants have exactly the values they must have for us to be here, conscious and alive.

It is as if you were standing 10 feet from a large, white wall covered with a grid of half-inch squares, six of which have been chosen at random and painted red. You are then blindfolded, given six darts in one hand, and told to throw the darts at the wall in one go. You do so, remove your blindfold, and discover to your astonishment that each of the six darts has landed inside one of the six red squares.

What would you make of this? Surely you would reject the idea of chance and insist that somehow, someone must have engineered it. The likelihood of this occurring randomly is so remotely tiny that it may as well be zero. There must be more than meets the eye.

This is the problem faced by scientists and theologians. What is going on?

Some Christians insist that this "more than meets the eye" is God, who, they say, has, by adjusting these six numbers, tuned the universe as a mechanic might tune a car—carefully, so that it runs and moves in the way the mechanic desires. This position is held by some advocates of intelligent design, who see evidence of intention and purpose in the tuning.

Meanwhile, scientists have suggested their own solution: the multiverse.

This word "multiverse" admits a host of distinct definitions. Sometimes it describes causally disconnected regions of our one universe. Sometimes it arises within certain interpretations of quantum mechanics. Sometimes it refers to cyclic, serial universes that arise one after another over time. Other meanings also exist. We will use multiverse to mean a vast ensemble of individual universes, each as real as the next, each disconnected from the others, each identified by its own set of physical constants. No two universes within this multiverse share the same set of six numbers; therefore, no two are identical in structure, lifetime, number of dimensions, density, etc.

Under this scenario all possible universes are realized, and of course we ourselves occupy one of the relatively few in which life as we know it is possible. The existence of our unique, tuned-for-life universe is no more surprising than the existence of a winning lottery ticket. Both are inevitable.

If this sounds like science fiction, that is because it nearly is. Now, to be fair, some variants of certain cosmological theories are suggestive of the multiverse. The concept was not originally created by scientists as a way to avoid bringing God (or an intelligent designer) into the discussion. But this particular conception of the multiverse, and of life's inevitability along with it, has definitely seen an uptick in popularity ever since the sheer improbability of our fine-tuned universe has come to light.

So, on one hand we have theologians and intelligent design advocates solving the problem of the fine-tuned universe with God. On the other hand, we have scientists solving it with a practically infinite ensemble of universes.

If I were forced to choose between the two, I'd pick God because it is the simplest solution. *Occam's razor* is a problem-solving principle that says, when deciding between two hypotheses that give rise to the same phenomena, you should pick the one that requires fewer assumptions. The simplest explanation tends to be the right one: I'd pick God.

But I don't choose this option because (a) I don't have to, and (b) the God of intelligent design is not the God of my understanding. The God of my understanding does not tinker or tune. The God of my understanding is not particularly anthropomorphic, and I am deeply suspicious of all language that makes the Creator seem like a big invisible person. To say that God carefully set the values of six physical constants at the time of the big bang and then sat back and let it rip violates my sense of both the immanence and transcendence of God. Many people have no trouble with talking about God this way, but for me it simply does not compute. I prefer not to use God as the solution to a scientific problem.

I also reject the multiverse. To be clear, I do not reject *all* models of the multiverse. In particular, I support the notion of causally disconnected regions of our one actual universe that act effectively as separate universes. But I cannot say that the multiverse described above, comprising an infinitude of disconnected universes, each bearing a distinct set of physical constants, each as real as the next, represents a serious scientific idea. It is not serious because it is not falsifiable. What data could ever reject it? It may be consistent with physics as we know it, but mere consistency does not drive science. Ultimately there must be empirical evidence for all scientific claims, and so far as I can see, there is none forthcoming for this one.

Theologically, I am opposed to the God solution; scientifically, I am opposed to the multiverse solution. Which lands me right where I am: content to not know the answer today, happy to have the problem to work on, and hopeful for a solution in the future.

One of these solutions might be found in the physical constants themselves. Today physicists see no connections between these six numbers, and there may be none. But, on the other hand, there may be such a connection. Physics has come a long way over the last century, and we never know what we have yet to learn. It may be that these constants are all related and could not be other than they are. Perhaps what we call contingent is in fact necessary.

Or perhaps we simply lack imagination. Life as we know it is no more than life as we know it. Maybe human beings could not survive in other universes, but other forms of life could. Maybe life as we *don't* know it could exist across a broad range of universes. If this is the case, then it would not be so surprising that some kind of life—*our* kind of life—is here, in the one and only universe, today.

Question 32

If you invited your congregation into your classroom, what topic would you cover?

The most memorable teaching experience I have ever had took place some years ago in Dharamsala, India, where I served on the faculty of the Emory-Tibet Science Initiative, a partnership between Emory University and His Holiness the 14th Dalai Lama. The goal of the program was to incorporate science into the curriculum for Tibetan Buddhist monastics. For several summers I traveled with a group of professors to the seat of the exiled Tibetan government to teach science to the monks.

During the second summer I was assigned to teach Einstein's theory of relativity. I presented the subject to my cohort of monks, using little to no mathematics. I told them about the theory, outlined its basic results, and described experiments that have verified it. Eyebrows were raised, questions were asked, and after class two students approached me from the front row. One of them smiled and said, in a respectful and direct manner, "The theory is not correct." I asked him to explain. He replied with great seriousness: "This is not how time works, and this is not how space works. The theory contradicts what is real." It remains to this day both the most emphatic and most polite rejection of science I have ever seen.

I was surprised (and amused) at the courtesy and matter-of-factness with which the monk rejected relativity, but I was not surprised that he found it strange. Relativity, our standard theory of space, time, and gravity, is difficult to wrap your head around. But it can be taught without a lot of mathematics, and, once understood, its predictions, which have been confirmed to as many decimal places as we can measure, consistently evoke disbelief from those who encounter them for the first time. The monk from the front row was just one of many people who have found relativity hard to believe.

Einstein's famous theory rejects some of your most fundamental assumptions about the world, assumptions so basic that you almost certainly don't know you have them. For example, you probably assume that time rolls forward at a nice even pace for everyone in the universe, that everyone ages at the same rate, and that every clock ticks once per second for everyone. But this is not right. Time is flexible, and its rate of flow depends on how fast you're moving and on the strength of your local gravity field, among other things. Space also depends on these factors. You probably assume that the straight-line distance between two points—say, your house and the closest grocery store—is the same for everyone in the universe, that everyone can agree on it. This is also incorrect. Space is stretchy. Neither time nor space is absolute. They are, instead, relative.

One of the most mind-bending consequences is that two twins may find themselves with different ages. Suppose that, on your 30th birthday, your twin climbs aboard a rocket and flies off to a planet orbiting a nearby star at 99% light speed. She makes it to the planet, takes care of business, and returns to Earth at the same speed. Relativity says that, upon her return, she will be younger than you. How much younger depends on how far away the other planet is and therefore how long the trip lasted, but she could easily be many years younger. She will look at you and wonder why you look so old, and you will look at her and wonder how she managed to age so little. This age-warping effect is not science fiction. The only thing that stands in the way of us actually experiencing something like this is the yet-to-be-developed technology to get a rocket moving so fast.

My students often ask, "But how can it be this way?" My answer is that, if we routinely moved much faster than we do, or if the speed of light were much less than it is, we would all be aware of the flexibility of time and space and we would all see that that's just the way things are. In other words, relativity is just the way the universe operates and the only reason it seems strange to us is that it lies outside of our experience.

Importantly, this relativity of space and time is necessary for the laws of physics to be *not* relative. What led Einstein down the path toward relativity was his insistence that the laws of physics be the same for all people everywhere—that is, absolute. But for these laws to be absolute, space and time had to be relative in exactly the way they turned out to be. So, in a nice ironic turn, it was his faith in the absolute that led Einstein to relativity.

You may wonder why, when I have so many lessons I could teach, I would choose to teach relativity to my congregation. Why not teach evolution, with all its theological implications?

First, I have taught physics at the college level for more than 20 years, and relativity is the subject I most love to teach. It's easy and pleasurable to teach when you are enamored with the subject. You may have memories of subjects in which you had little to no interest upon entering the class, but the enthusiasm of the teacher brought the subject alive for you.

Second, relativity makes us question our fundamental ideas about the universe. In this way it is like the Copernican theory, which, 500 years ago, forced a similar renegotiation. It is hard to imagine how disorienting it must have been for people who had assumed all their lives that the earth was fixed and immovable. Scientists were the first to deal with a sun-centered universe, but eventually everyone else had to also. It may be that in some distant future, everyone will know relativity! But I choose it not for this reason, but because I love big ideas that force us to question our everyday assumptions.

Finally, the moral of relativity, as of so much of science, is this: Our experience and knowledge are limited, the world is often not as it seems, and we do not know our neighborhood as well as we suppose. "Our life is a faint tracing on the surface of mystery," writes Annie Dillard in *Pilgrim at Tinker Creek*.[1] "Nothing is rich but the inexhaustible wealth of nature. She shows us only surfaces, but she is a million fathoms deep," wrote Ralph Waldo Emerson in one of his many letters.[2] If these things are true, and relativity is just one sign that they are, then what are we Christians to do? How are we to think about a creator who creates such a cosmos, with surprises lurking one after another beyond our vision? And how can we presume to know so much when our perception is so limited? How can we place confidence in our theology when science, which is in many ways simpler than theology, is so often revealed to be incomplete?

My hope is that such questions, taken seriously, will not so much cause us to lose faith as they will engender humility. It is right and proper and good to believe, and to take belief seriously; but it is at some point necessary to hold beliefs lightly, with a sense of humor, wonder, and trust in the goodness of God. We see through a glass darkly, wrote the apostle Paul, and relativity, a seminal breakthrough in human vision, stands, ironically, as one reminder of this our finite frame.

Notes

[1] Annie Dillard, *Pilgrim at Tinker Creek* (Harper Collins, 1974), 17.
[2] www.bartleby.com/90/0804.html.

Question 33
Skepticism is important to the progress of science, but what role, if any, does skepticism play in the life of faith?

Father McCafferty asked, "Why do you believe what you believe?" This question was put to me and my fellow high school juniors with great emphasis by the old Irish Marist priest, our philosophy teacher. This was a Catholic high school, so he eventually got around to God. "Do you believe in God?" he asked us sharply. "And if you do, why? Do you believe in God because your parents believe in God?"

It was one of my first forays into the world of serious questions, and I was thrilled that they were asked out loud and discussed freely. Father McCafferty's questions resonated with me and excited me with the prospect of learning by digging down into my own viewpoint, of questioning myself, of testing my perspective. My natural skepticism, my tendency to ask a lot of questions, had lain dormant until then. Father McCafferty was the first teacher to give it the green light.

Skepticism is not cynicism. It is not just a bad mood. Skepticism is a posture of persistent questioning, doubt, and uncertainty. It seeks not to burn everything down but rather to find ideas and approaches that work. Skepticism is a search for what's real.

Scientists place great value on skepticism. Without it, scientific progress stalls, discoveries remain hidden, and old limited or incorrect ideas persist. The habit of questioning constitutes a great part of scientific integrity, and it is every scientist's responsibility to question not only others' theories but also their own—especially their own. "A scientist's first principle is that you must not fool yourself, and you are the easiest person to fool," said American physicist Richard Feynman in his 1974 commencement speech at the California Institute of Technology. "I'm talking about a specific, extra type of integrity that is not lying, but bending over backwards to show how you're maybe wrong, [an integrity] that you ought to have when acting as a scientist." So, scientists must be skeptical in general, but their skepticism should be particularly focused on their own observations, experiments, and results. Eventually, Feynman said, "the truth will come out. Other experimenters will repeat your experiment and find out whether you were wrong or right."*

But clearly marked bounds place limits on scientific skepticism, which does not apply to all things under the sun. For example, you will never hear a scientist, speaking as a scientist, turn her skepticism back on the scientific method itself. She will not, as a scientist, be skeptical of her scientific skepticism, because once she starts critiquing the general method of science, she is no longer doing science: she has delved into philosophy. Scientific skepticism is not a universal acid. It stays in its lane—purposeful, focused, controlled, directed only at the objects of

---

*See calteches.library.caltech.edu/51/2/CargoCult.htm.

scientific inquiry: physical and biological features of the universe and scientific theories about them.

The role of skepticism in Christian life is less clear. On one hand, you must question what you have been told in order to grow up. Children in religious families are taught to believe a great number of unbelievable things, many of which show up in the first few pages of their Bibles: six-day creation, talking serpents, forbidden fruit, a global flood, all those animals on a boat, and so forth.

At some point most children ask questions, and many of these questions have answers. For example, the answer to the question asked by so many 12-year-olds, "Was there really a talking snake?" is "no." And beyond this *no* lies a whole world of biblical scholarship, theology, poetry, and meaning, waiting to be pursued by any who care to know more. This *no* is easily contained within the bounds of orthodox Christianity.

On the other hand, how long can this continue? We can say with confidence that the words of Genesis 1–3 do not pass the test of historical, scientific accuracy, and we can rest there if we choose. But some are more curious than others, and press on: Were Adam and Eve real? How about Abraham and David? How about the prophets? How about Jesus? And did all those miracles really happen? And if those people weren't real and if those miracles—in particular, the miracle of the Resurrection—didn't happen, what are we talking about here?

Lots of work has been done on these questions also, but the waters get deeper and clear answers grow scarce as you go. Not only that, but this kind of skepticism brings you up against the boundaries of Christianity, for the faith of many people stands or falls upon the Resurrection. Perhaps questioning the Resurrection is out-of-bounds for Christian skepticism, as is questioning the scientific method out-of-bounds for scientific skepticism. You are perfectly free to be skeptical about the scientific method: but when you are, you are no longer acting as a scientist. And you are perfectly free to be skeptical about the Resurrection: but when you are, you are no longer acting as a Christian.

This is the perspective of many believers, and they have scripture to support their boundaries. "If Christ has not been raised, then our proclamation has been in vain and your faith has been in vain," writes Paul in 1 Cor. 15:14. Others have longer lists of non-negotiables: the virgin birth, other miracles, the historicity of the whole New Testament. Still others claim that, if you do not believe in the literal, historical, physical accuracy of the entire Bible—starting with Gen. 1:1 and ending with Rev. 22:21—then you are not a Christian. But nearly every Christian holds some belief or set of beliefs that, if shown to be false, would bring down their faith.

This being said, I for one believe that skepticism is one way to love God with all your mind. But please note, and this is of absolute importance: Your questions must be *your* questions. They cannot be questions asked by other people. They cannot be the mere fashion of the day. You must own them. They must spring from your mind and your heart as truly as any thought or desire ever does. And if your questions scare you, then you must ask them. You should present your questions to God and to the world as a prayer, as an expression of your humanity and of your God-given desire to know and understand. And when answers come, however they come, you can begin to stand on your own small patch of solid ground.

The skeptic's journey of faith is for the skeptic. It is not for everyone. But for me, for Fr. McCafferty, and many others, it is the only way to be true.

Finally, I would like to put in a good word for trust. We believe many things on simple trust. For example, how do you know that the earth goes around the sun? I'm not asking for appeals to authority; I'm asking, "What evidence do you have?" The answer is that you have none. No experience, no evidence of your senses, no chain of reasoning guides your conclusion. You believe it because someone—probably your 3rd grade teacher—told you it was true. And that's fine. Most of what we believe, we believe because it was told to us by someone we trusted. What I would like to suggest, however, is that if we rely too much on that kind of knowledge, we could find in the end that we have never really learned anything.

The love of God, our tradition, and our own personal faith do not rely on our denial of our true questions. Paul wrote, "For I am convinced that neither death, nor life, nor angels, nor rulers, nor things present, nor things to come, nor powers, nor height, nor depth, nor anything else in all creation, will be able to separate us from the love of God in Christ Jesus our Lord" (Rom. 8:38-39). I believe Paul would include our questions and our doubts on this list.

Question 34

If you could add one scientific idea into the language of the church, what would it be?

I was a sophomore at Young Harris College when I first learned about the total solar eclipse of 2017. Jimmy Westlake, our astronomy professor, told us it was coming and would even be visible from campus. We laughed: in 1987, "2017" didn't even sound like a year. But he went on, telling us that not only was the eclipse to take place on Monday, August 21, but that, as seen from campus, the total phase would begin at 2:36:07 pm and would end precisely at 2:38:30 pm. He told us it was inevitable, a mathematical certainty. Again, this was 30 years before the event itself. I put the date on my calendar and got on with my life.

Ten addresses, three degrees, five jobs, one wedding, 26 years of marriage, and three kids later: Monday, August 21, 2017 arrived. My wife Elizabeth and I took the children out of school and left Atlanta for the mountains of North Georgia where, at about noon, we joined a happy throng of students on the Young Harris quad. We waited and stood and watched. At 2:36:07 the moon completed its long slide over the sun and darkness fell. Venus and Mars appeared. Birds fell silent and a cool wind blew across the weirdly-lit world. Exactly two minutes and 23 seconds later the edge of the sun emerged, blue like burning phosphorus, and the world slowly returned to full light. It all happened just as Professor Westlake had told us three decades earlier, and precisely, exactly on time.

This kind of certainty is rare in the world, and a great part of that day's joy derived from the fact that I had known it was coming, and right *when* it was coming, and I had known it for so long. This exact certain knowledge, manifested as it was in such a politically and socially uncertain time, struck me as a thing of fabulous beauty. It still does. It makes me feel safe. It assures me that, underneath everything, the world makes sense.

We all need fixed points to stabilize our lives. They keep us from guessing all the time. We rely on our planners and calendars and weekly cycles. We like to know how our days will go, what to expect. Routines keep us happy and safe. Every year we find peace in the traditions of Advent and Lent, and the holy hopeful days of Christmas and Easter. These and other annual seasons and days mark time predictably, regularly, soothingly. Order is very good; creation itself is a triumph of order out of chaos.

But the chaos, as we all know, was never completely vanquished. It remains all around us and within us, threatening to undo us still. Seas swell and winds blow. And sometimes winds grow into storms and we latch hard onto handles of belief and habit that in easier times we would hold lightly. Not all these handles prove to be stable, unfortunately. Some of them, unlike Newtonian physics, are mere figments of our need and end up failing us. Some of them are not designed to withstand so much stress. In such times we seek something nearly impossible to find under the sun: certitude.

A large portion of the American church has fallen into such a situation. The political and social tempests of the last 50 years have caused many churchgoers to seek the solace of certitude, some impenetrable shelter of assurance and truth and comfort.

This longing for certitude takes on many forms. In the face of social upheaval and uncertainty, a large segment of the church holds ever tighter to such fixed notions as young earth, six-day creationism. Fiery, hard-edged rules about who is righteous and who is not have gained dominance. And, most distressingly, a large fraction of American Christians has sold out the faith for political expediency and social control.

A mountain of clear evidence stands against six-day creationism, yet this belief persists in our churches, evolving into ever-more-fervent forms. Suspicion and fear of people who are not white, Christian, and straight has driven churches inward, setting them against the world and turning the good news into bad news for everyone outside their walls. The recent betrayal of the church to the powers and principalities that would eliminate all dissent is a grievous episode in American religious history.

These Christians' beliefs and actions are grounded in firm certitude about scripture, the nature of creation, the lines between ingroups and outgroups, and the righteousness of their own religious and political will. Surely this segment of the church views uncertainty as a liability.

It is for this reason that, if I were to introduce a scientific idea into the language of the church, it would be the "uncertainty principle." This law of physics, first derived by German physicist Werner Heisenberg in 1927, rests at the foundations of quantum mechanics, our physical theory that governs tiny objects such as atoms and their nuclei.

I will not dive deeply into the uncertainty principle, which has to do with simultaneous measurements of certain pairs of physical quantities, but suffice it to say that this principle tells us the uncertainty in science is not just an effect of our imperfect lab equipment or our limited research budgets. It tells us there are in-principle, inescapable limits to what we can possibly know about the universe, and no amount of money or clever lab hacks can get around them. These limits do not play a major role in the Newtonian physics of big objects such as the sun and moon, but they play an enormous role at the atomic and subatomic levels, and we have them to thank for the large-scale structure of the universe.

The universe is an uncertain place, and there is nothing we can do about that. Absolute certainty doesn't exist anywhere, not even in Newtonian physics. It is no more than an expression of our longing. Taking this simple truth out of labs and classrooms and into the church might have some powerful and positive effects.

First, it would encourage us to stop clinging so desperately to things that are not real, that hurt people, and that compromise the gospel. The picture in the minds of young earth creationists exists nowhere else but in their minds. It does not correspond to anything in reality. Christians are everywhere and always called to let go of such unrealities, and even a little uncertainty can help everyone go a long way toward this end.

If Christians were to welcome a little uncertainty into their views of others, they might come to see that Jesus called us precisely to love and honor those who are marginalized, powerless, and unfamiliar. Jesus' enemies stood among those whose power and social position he threatened, and never, not once, among those on the margins of decent society. These days in America, Jesus would find wide acceptance among immigrants, sexual minorities, racial minorities, and so forth—the very people so many Christians have lined up against. To drop all need for certainty for one minute and simply ask the question, "Did Jesus love and accept the same people I do?" would be a new beginning for the American church.

One moment of real uncertainty about the church's political commitments could work wonders. Does it further the gospel to tie the church to a political agenda that demonizes people? That trafficks in fear? That is grounded in falsehood and deception? I cannot imagine the amount of damage that American Christianity's fetish for political power has done to the message of Jesus Christ. It is incalculable.

Many Christians, of course, do not cling to certainty about their theology, their relations with others, and their attachments to political figures. They allow themselves to be uncertain, to ask questions, to think critically about their own thoughts, actions, and commitments. But too many may allow themselves no such freedom. They cling to their own dream of certainty, to the ruin of many. And the uncertainty principle, rightly translated into the theology and practice of the American church, would be a gift not only to the church but also to the world.

Question 35
If you leave this life, enter the pearly gates, and are allowed to ask God one scientific question, what would you ask?

The question I would put to the Creator, and without hesitation, is this: Why quantum mechanics? Nearly a century has passed since Erwin Schrödinger proposed his famous equation that ushered in quantum mechanics, which is the physics of very small things. Well, Schrödinger's equation is famous among physicists, anyway, and it heralded a new and strange understanding of the world. So new and strange, in fact, was the theory and its implications that Schrödinger himself later remarked, "I don't like it and I'm sorry I ever had anything to do with it."*

What was the great Austrian physicist so worked up about? To answer this question, imagine that you are standing at the end of a pool table with a single billiard ball in your hand. You place the ball on the table and push it forward so that it bounces off the far cushion, returns to your side, bounces off the near cushion, and returns to the far side and bounces back again, back and forth. Now make two simple assumptions: (1) The ball moves directly toward and away from you so that it never hits a side cushion. (2) This is a frictionless table, so that once the ball begins moving it won't stop until you reach down and grab it. These assumptions are unrealistic, but they only serve to make things simple, so you will see how weird quantum mechanics is. (Ironically, physics deals in unreal, simple idealizations such as the frictionless table. But these idealizations are precisely what make physics so useful in the real world.)

And there you stand, watching your billiard ball bounce back and forth and back and forth along its path—toward you, away from you, toward you, away from you, all day long. Yes, it's a little boring, but please notice three things: (1) At any given time you can tell me where the ball is and how fast it's going. (2) The ball can go any speed you like, including no speed at all, depending on how hard you push it. (3) It can have only one speed: the speed you give it at the beginning. Again, none of these are interesting points. This is just the way things work.

But what would happen if we made the whole thing smaller—and by smaller, I mean *much* smaller? What if we shrunk the pool table down to the size of an atom and the ball to the size of a proton? In that case, quantum mechanics tells us that all three of the boring, unsurprising things listed above are no longer true.

You can no longer know simultaneously where the ball is and how fast it's moving. If you want to locate the ball precisely, then you lose all information about its speed. And if you want to know its speed, then you lose all information about its location. You can know the ball's speed or location, but not both. Knowledge of

---

*See www.nytimes.com/2005/12/26/science/a-quantum-sampler.html.

one comes *only* at the expense of knowledge of the other. This loss of information is not a matter of imperfect observations or measuring devices but is an absolute, in-principle limit built into the world. (For those keeping score, this limit is one consequence of something called the "Heisenberg Uncertainty Principle.")

Additionally, the tiny ball cannot go at any speed you like. Or perhaps I should put it this way: You can push the ball at any speed you like, but it almost certainly won't have that speed when you measure it. In fact, if you measure it, you will only find certain speeds and no others. As a simple example, suppose you push the ball at 7 mph, but when you measure it, you find it moving at 5 mph. So, you measure it again and find it again at 5—and again. But then you measure it a fourth time and find that now it's moving at 10 mph! You never touched it; you just measured its speed, and now it's moving faster. Then you check it again, and it's back at 5 mph.

Quantum mechanics tells us that only certain values of the speed are available to the ball. Perhaps in this case the ball can only have speeds that are multiples of 5 mph. You will never find the speed to be any number other than 5 or 10 or 15 or 20 or 25 mph, and so on. Other speeds are simply prohibited by the physics of the thing. You will never measure its speed to be 9 or 27 mph, say, even if you push it with a speed of 9 or 27 mph. Notice that I did not include zero in my list of possible speeds, because according to quantum mechanics it is impossible for the ball to be at rest. It just can't happen! You can place it on the table at rest, but when you measure its speed, you will never get zero.

Moreover—and this is what got Schrödinger all hot and bothered—the ball can go both 5 and 10 mph at the same time. But when you measure it, it must pick one of these values. You will never measure it going 5 *and* 10 mph, but you will always measure it going 5 *or* 10. But it really was going both speeds at once before you measured it, and the act of measuring forced it to pick one of its two options.

The ball and table are now behaving in ways that make no sense, and all we ever did was make them small.

To shine a light on the ridiculous nature of this last situation, of the ball going both 5 and 10 mph simultaneously, Schrödinger invented a famous thought experiment involving a cat in a box with a vial of poisonous gas. The vial is rigged to a switch that has a 50-50 chance of flipping over a 24-hour period. (Don't worry about what causes the switch to flip or not flip; just know that it has that 50/50 chance of flipping over a day's time.) If the switch flips, then the vial opens and the cat dies; if the switch does not flip, the cat remains alive (but perhaps a bit cramped and cranky).

So we put the cat in the box with the vial. We close the lid and start our one-day countdown. The next day we wait and watch nervously as the clock ticks down. At the instant it hits zero we go to the box. Is the cat alive or dead? Both scenarios have a 50% chance of being realized. With fear and trembling, we open the box. Behold! The cat is alive! (I love cats, and I don't like to kill them.)

Return now to the tiny ball and table. Recall that the ball can go both 5 *and* 10 mph at the same time, but when you measure its speed, it snaps into one of these two distinct possibilities. The act of measuring it forces the ball's speed to attain one of its two available values. Schrodinger said this situation is just as ridiculous as a cat who, with a 50/50 chance of being alive or dead, is in reality both alive and dead until we opened the box to "measure" the state of the cat and found it to be alive. According to the logic of quantum mechanics, the cat is truly in a mixed state of being both alive and dead until we open the box to look, and when we do this the cat snaps into one of its two available states: alive! The act of measuring Schrödinger's cat, and not what happened over those 24 hours, seals its fate.

This of course makes no sense, and neither Schrödinger nor anyone else believes that any cat has ever been simultaneously dead and alive, inside or outside any box. But our tiny ball *does* simultaneously move at 5 and 10 mph, and something makes it decide on one value or the other when we measure its speed. Quantum mechanics is just that weird.

This short essay barely touches on everything that could be said about the strangeness of quantum physics, but I hope it helps you see why, if I were given the chance to ask God one question about science, it would be: *Why quantum mechanics?*

Afterword*
A conversation about reconciling faith and science

NFJ: Regarding *Love and Quasars: An Astrophysicist Reconciles Faith and Science* (Fortress Press, 2019), how does this book differ from your first one?

PW: To see how *Love and Quasars* differs, I should first say how it is the same. It, like *Stars Beneath Us*, attempts to reconcile faith and science. But it does so in a completely new way. *Stars Beneath Us* is really an extended meditation of the biblical book of Job and therefore approaches the question through the universal human experience of suffering. It takes a rather dark and indirect look at the perennial questions of faith and science and in some ways leaves the issue unresolved, just as the question of suffering is itself unresolved in Job.

Love and Quasars, however, is a direct answer to a direct question. In 2018 a student found out that I'm a minister as well as a physics professor. She stopped still in the hall and stared at me hard. You could nearly see the question mark floating over her head. "How does THAT work?" she asked.

Love and Quasars is my answer, written as simply and directly as possible. In contrast to *Stars Beneath Us*, it approaches the question of faith and science through the universal human experience of love. It is simpler, more direct, and offers an actual resolution to the problem. It is written on a simpler level, with more direct language and less poetics. It is brighter and more joyful and optimistic. But it was harder to write because, for me, darker topics are often easier to address. So, *Love and Quasars* feels like a bigger risk to me personally.

NFJ: I wish all books, especially the Bible, began with: "Introduction: What this book is about and how it works." Why did you start *Love and Quasars* in such a way?

PW: Because I worked hard to make the book simple, user-friendly, direct, and structured, starting right up front with the introduction. I believe, as author Brené Brown puts it, that "clarity is kind."

NFJ: You advocate for an evolving faith when, in fact, most of us were encouraged to have a strong faith. Is part of the problem that "strong" was interpreted as "rigid," not allowing for needed critical analysis and change?

PW: Yes! This is an important distinction. If early Christians had valued rigid faith over strong faith, Christianity would have crumbled centuries ago. To not collapse in an earthquake or storm, skyscrapers must be flexible. Bones have strength because

---

*Adapted from an interview published in *Nurturing Faith Journal* (January/February, 2020).

they bend. To survive in a changing world, life must evolve. All of this is true for ideas and practices as well: they must grow and develop and change, or they will die. What is sometimes not appreciated is that this can happen while maintaining and even deepening the roots of faith.

NFJ: You write that, during high school and college, you thought you had to choose between faith and science. How does the church create that unnecessary dilemma, and what is a more constructive approach?

PW: Overall, today's church seems to be better at providing answers than it is at developing questions. Answers are not unimportant, but you have to work for them. Answers that come too easily act like patches: they cover the territory temporarily but don't address the deeper needs.

Teenagers, for example, have flexible, adept minds and can memorize and quote answers quite easily. Sometimes it's good to have an answer, even though you don't really understand it. But if we don't allow teens to take ultimate responsibility for their answers, their faith's roots will remain shallow and they'll wither at the least challenge. Like the building that won't flex because it's not built correctly, they will crumble. And there's no way to get to the point of strength with flexibility without asking a lot of questions and sitting with them long enough to feel their urgency, which is uncomfortable for a lot of people. Teenage minds can handle uncertainty; adult church leaders need to handle it too.

NFJ: Related to that question, what have you discovered in teaching science to college students who come from a strong church background?

PW: I have had very few students, if any, come to me conflicted about faith and science. This may be a function of what I teach (physics, which most students don't have a problem with) and where I teach it (an almost completely secular institution).

NFJ: Your book is filled with personal stories and analogies rather than exclusively scientific theories and theological jargon. I find it effective, but why did you choose this approach?

PW: I am above all else a teacher, so I'm interested in reaching people who are not experts. If you need jargon to teach a topic, then you're not really teaching it. Translation of technical scientific and theological language into everyday terms leads to a loss of some nuance—which is unavoidable—but to reach a larger audience, you need to be willing to suffer that loss for the sake of others. A writer must begin where the reader actually is. I strive to remain aware of my audience and what they do and don't know.

NFJ: Your résumé is impressive, but shouldn't "household dinosaur expert" get more prominence? How did that childhood obsession impact a church-going kid?

PW: It made me pretty sure that God was larger and stranger than I could imagine. If God so loved the world, as I was taught, and if dinosaurs were part of the world, which they very much were to me, then God must have loved the dinosaurs. This is not a thought many people consider very seriously, but I thought about it quite a lot—and quite seriously—as a child. It opens up your view of God.

NFJ: You give specific examples in the book, but how in general does the way the Bible is approached either harm or help in reconciling faith and science?

PW: The more you insist that scripture, and Genesis in particular, is historically accurate, the more trouble you will have with what science has to say to us. This goes back to the issue of rigidity and strength from your previous question. Genesis 1, for example, is a straightforward description of God creating a flat earth. Now we know, despite some people who claim otherwise, that the earth is spherical. So, how rigidly do you plan to hold to a literal surface-level reading of that book? You just can't do it, and no one actually does it. If the Bible were meant to be a science book, we'd have thrown it out centuries ago.

In my experience the most helpful way to read Genesis is relationally. Three major players—God, humanity, and creation—are introduced, and three relationships are established. These relationships are God-humanity, humanity-creation, and God-creation. Once they are in place all three relationships are ruptured, and much of the rest of scripture is an account of God's (and our) attempts to restore them. When you read the Bible in this way, the whole question of how the world was made—creation versus evolution—becomes much less urgent and also less complicated: the possibility of both/and opens up, whereas before there was only either/or.

NFJ: How much of an obstacle to healthy faith-science understandings are young earth creationists such as Ken Ham of "Answers in Genesis," whom you mention in your book? Isn't it odd that those who call for a strong faith actually appear to have a very fragile faith that can't withstand scientific discovery?

PW: I think they're a huge obstacle and hugely off-putting to many young people who might otherwise be attracted to Christianity. Ham, for example, is focused on one thing above all: being right. His organization is called Answers in Genesis, and it really is all about answers—the perfect, right ones. Of course, it's nice to be right occasionally, and none of us want to go through life making error after error, but their emphasis on the right answers seems to admit no room for grace, creativity, or real dialogue. I know several people personally who, once they realized they didn't have to reject science to be a Christian, felt a great burden fall from their shoulders. My only comfort is that, as I mentioned above, such a rigid brand of faith really can't flourish too long on a large scale.

NFJ: You are also critical of atheists who treat the Bible in the same way they approach science. What do you mean by the statement "When science lines up against faith, it makes its own mess"?

PW: Oftentimes scientists see faith—including the Bible—as little more than science done badly. For them, science stands as the one true source of knowledge and all other ways of knowing have value only insofar as they mimic science. Now some points of overlap exist between faith and science, and I talk about them in the book, but they really are distinct ways of knowing the world. Compressing faith into a box called "science" does it no justice, and neither is it helpful to say things such as "it really takes faith to believe in science," because that is just making the opposite mistake.

NFJ: Despite your vast scientific understanding—which few of us share—you often reference simple encounters with nature, such as walking in the woods and bird watching, as bringing you meaning. It doesn't take much, does it?

PW: No, it doesn't, but I would never say that my knowledge of physics and astronomy doesn't have a powerful effect when I'm out in the field birding. It sits in the background to be sure, but it's not unimportant. What a full scientific education will do for you is make you appreciative of every single facet of the natural world. I know a little physics and astronomy, and I don't use the word "little" in a self-deprecating sense. I'm simply stating a fact: there is so much more to know, even in my own field. How much more then do I not know about biology, a much larger discipline and one that I have not studied formally since high school? How much do I not know about geology? About chemistry? About atmospheric science? About the ocean? About birds?

So, when I go birding all this awareness of not-knowing is sitting just under the surface, and it makes me feel like creation is a cathedral I could explore my whole life and for many lifetimes beyond that. It makes seeing something new so much more exciting, like a true and lovely gift!

NFJ: If a church, college, theology school, or other group wanted you to speak about these issues, how would they contact you?

PW: They can reach me at pwallace.net, and I will get back to them directly.

www.ingramcontent.com/pod-product-compliance
Lightning Source LLC
Chambersburg PA
CBHW030906170426
43193CB00009BA/749